THE END OF THE COLD WAR?

THE END OF THE COLD WAR?

Thomas W. Simons, Jr.

ST. MARTIN'S PRESS
New York

First published in the United States of America in 1990.

Printed in the United States of America.

ISBN 0-312-04536-0

Library of Congress Cataloging-in-Publication Data

Simons, Thomas W.
      The end of the cold war? / Thomas W. Simons, Jr.
          p. cm.
      ISBN 0-312-04536-0
      1. Cold War. 2. Peace. I. Title.
D849.S59 1990
909.82—dc20   90-32508
                                                          CIP

To my family, and to my friends and
colleagues on the EUR oar deck

In Boston serpents whistle at the cold.
The victim climbs the altar steps and sings:
"Hosannah to the lion, lamb and beast
Who fans the furnace-face of IS with wings:
I breathe the ether of my marriage feast."
At the high altar, gold
And a fair cloth. I kneel and the wings beat
My cheek. What can the dove of Jesus give
You now but wisdom, exile? Stand and live,
The dove has brought an olive branch to eat.

— **ROBERT LOWELL,**
Where the Rainbow Ends

Contents

Preface

This book is based on Seven Lectures on the End of the Cold War, which I delivered between September 26 and October 25, 1989, under the auspices of the Stephen A. Ogden, Jr. Memorial Lecture Series on International Affairs at Brown University. Editing has been confined largely to redundancies, so this text is still substantially as delivered, a record of the spoken word.

It therefore retains the informality and what I hope will prove to be the accessibility of the original talks. By the same token, however, it does not pretend to scholarly rigor. It was written in a little over three months, between my last day on the job as the American Deputy Assistant Secretary of State responsible for U.S. relations with the Soviet Union, Eastern Europe, and Yugoslavia, on June 2, 1989, and the first lecture September 26. While I am satisfied that my own notes and recollections give it a fully accurate factual base, it is without the references and footnotes that genuine scholarship on this turbulent period will surely require.

At the same time I have tried to make it more than simply an early commentary on very recent events. I would like it to be a work of history, no more — but also no less — than a serious, coherent, chronological account of how East-West relations developed during the 1980s.

The period between my entry on duty as Director for Soviet Union Affairs in the Department of State on August 3, 1981, and my departure in June 1989 provides the natural core. In describing it I could draw on my experience as a participant in the American policy process and an official with responsibilities in U.S. relations with the Soviet Union and the European Communist states. What follows is thus primarily an account of policy development in West and East, and it focuses most closely on American policy. This is partly because Soviet and East European policies were even more mysterious, but mainly because American policy is what I know best. Yet this is not a Washington insider's account in the classic sense of an explanation of policy development framed largely in terms of the titanic personal and bureaucratic battles being waged at any given moment within the Beltway. Even as an insider I was not privy to many facts that may in retrospect seem more important than those presented here. Often, however, I found that even the juiciest insider facts did not adequately explain what I saw and felt going on around me. In order to understand, I felt I needed a broader focus, one that goes farther back in time and farther out in geography without underestimating the critical importance of near-term political considerations for any (and almost every) specific development.

The historical approach came naturally. I was trained as a historian and have lived for years in countries whose leaders have tried to cram life into an imposed historicist framework. For those very reasons, however, I was aware of how easy it is to warp complex human and political realities by imposing large ideas on them. I knew that History with a capital H is as dangerous to real understanding as exclusive concentration on today's political agenda. Still, I felt the need for a larger approach, and still, for me, that approach could only be historical.

Such an approach does not have a great deal of practical value in the policy process. The moments when it does, when it provides a broad-gauge rationale for a major policy shift, as George Kennan did in his "Long Telegram" at the outset of the Cold War, are privileged and fondly recalled by historians. But they are also exceeding rare. One of my superiors once asked me why we weren't thinking about "these things" — larger trends and their larger significance. I replied that we were, but we tried not to let it interfere with our work. At the same time I found that the effort to take such an approach, respectful of yesterday and tomorrow as well as of the moment, was psychologically essential, and not unuseful to my work. And my current assignment as Diplomat-in-Residence at Brown University has given me the opportunity to apply it more consistently and systematically to the decade just past than was called for, or possible, while it was going on. This book is the result.

As history, this account begins before and extends past the 1980s. In the first and fifth chapters, on U.S.–Soviet relations and on the division of Europe as a problem for the international system up to the turn of the 1980s, I have sought to give what I consider the historical background needed for understanding the evolution of recent events. These analyses in turn draw partly on my reading, but mainly on my efforts over what is now more than a quarter century as a professional diplomat to comprehend the world in which I was working, through reflection. My historian's optimism that history can help also drew me modestly into the future.

Given the torrential pace of change in the East, there are advantages to a historical approach. The pace has picked up since I gave my lectures, and while it perplexes us all, it is terrifying to scholars who must try to fix the moment, and to their publishers. Trying in the main body of this work to consider the 1980s as history may make the work become obsolete less quickly than some other analyses. Still, some trends should be discernible from the experience of the decade, and in the last chapter I have tried both to stay close to the political realities as I see them and to extrapolate from them, to consider their potential long-range significance in light of the past. Here I have gone beyond "my decade" in office, up to the Bush administration's first step up from the policy legacy of its predecessor during the President's trip to Europe in May 1989, to suggest how the process of reform in Communist countries may evolve and what it could mean for all of us in the next century if it continues. But the focus is on the 1980s, a decade with a course and personality of its own. So although I hope it will cast light on the future, the aspiration of this book is not to predict the future but to stand as a work of history.

Acknowledgments

My intentions have been straightforward and historical, but the path that brought me to this point has been anything but straight, and a host of people and institutions helped and encouraged along the way. None of them share responsibility for the views I express here, and I am bound to say that those views do not necessarily reflect the views of the Department of State in particular. But I am grateful to them all. I owe a great deal to my father, who is also a trained historian and experienced American diplomat, and to my mother, who keeps the spirit of the first generation of American postwar diplomacy alive as if nothing had changed. When I was still on campus, and now that I am on campus again, I have found that I am peculiar in never having had any doubts about what I wanted to do and become when I grew up, if I possibly could. I owe even more to my wife and best friend, Peggy, who has rightly continued to insist that I grow up, and to our extraordinary children, Suzanne and Benjamin, who gave new meaning to the concept of "quality time" during the years of sixty- and seventy-hour work weeks that are one basis for the pages that follow.

The world will repay those who spent those work weeks with me in the Bureau of European and Canadian Affairs (EUR) of the Department of State and in our embassies and consulates general in Europe and the Soviet Union, more or less according to their just deserts. But I can never repay the debt of gratitude I feel for having been part of a fellowship of shared dedication, shared endeavor, and shared excellence. I have particularly in mind my colleagues in the Office of Soviet Union Affairs (SOV) and the Office of East European and Yugoslav Affairs (EEY), and the veterans of those offices with whom I worked and who are now spread across the world, in and out of the Foreign Service. Modest, intelligent, hardworking, crossgrained, patriotic, they are a credit to the United States and to American diplomacy, and a national asset. They helped make history, and for the better, for this country and, I am convinced, for mankind. I hope they recognize some of our accomplishment in this account.

I would also like to thank three institutions whose commodious spirit has given me the chance to develop and then to refine and articulate the ideas set forth in these pages: in Washington, the Kennan Institute of the Woodrow Wilson Center of the Smithsonian Institution, itself an institution almost unique in the world as an agora where policy and scholarship, freedom and discipline, meet and embrace, and in particular the director of its East European Program, Professor John Lampe; in Washington and worldwide, the Foreign Service of the United States, an unlikely but genuine haven for reflective people who also like to work hard, and in particular Director General George Vest, now retired, who suggested my Diplomat-in-Residence assignment to me last spring; and in Providence, Brown University, meaning the Center for Foreign Policy Development and its director, Mark Garrison, the Institute for International Studies and its director, Howard Swearer, the Department of History and its chairman, Abbott Gleason, and of course the Stephen A. Ogden, Jr. Memorial Lecture Series. I was not quite a stranger, and they still took me in.

Finally, I would like to thank my editor at St. Martin's Press, Simon Winder, for a combination of generosity and skill in handling a newcomer that still amazes me.

Abbreviations

ABM	anti-ballistic missile
ASEAN	Association of South-East Asian Nations
CSCE	Conference on Security and Cooperation in Europe
CMEA	Council on Mutual Economic Assistance
EEC	European Economic Community
GLCM	ground-launched cruise missile
ICBM	intercontinental ballistic missile
IMF	International Monetary Fund
INF	intermediate nuclear-range forces
MBFR	Mutual and Balanced Force Reduction
NATO	North Atlantic Treaty Organization
SALT	Strategic Arms Limitation Talks
SDI	Strategic Defense Initiative
SLBM	submarine-launched ballistic missile
START	Strategic Arms Reduction Talks

Chapter 1

The Roots of New Thinking in U.S.-Soviet Relations

I n U.S.-Soviet relations, the 1980s will have been the decade of Ronald Reagan and Mikhail Sergeievich Gorbachev, so it is well to start with them. In his meetings with President Reagan and other American leaders, Gorbachev generally makes a presentation on the current state of *perestroika*. He knows that they are interested, and he knows that their fix on the status and prospects of reform in the Soviet Union is an important ingredient in their own policy toward his country. He does not enjoy making these presentations, because putting one's domestic affairs on the diplomatic table could imply that the other fellow has some legitimate say in what you do at home. And in this case the other fellow is the other superpower, the United States, the country all those expensive missiles are aimed at, the country whose own missiles are aimed at you, the country, as all Soviets were taught to believe for generations, that leads the "imperialist camp." So Gorbachev makes these presentations because they are useful rather than because he enjoys them. Often he preempts questions, offers answers to questions the Americans have not yet asked. Taking notes, I thought to myself on such occasions that he must be volunteering these accounts before the Americans asked in order to avoid that uncomfortable implication that he was doing things at home to please *them*, and thereby impinging on Soviet sovereignty after seven decades of revolutionary effort by his party to secure it.

At any rate, on one of those occasions Gorbachev volunteered that talk about internal opposition to him and to *perestroika* was just that: talk. There was no opposition in that sense, he said. On the other hand, he said, every Soviet carried opposition to reform within himself or herself. It was that kind of opposition, the inertial resistance to change, to reform, the attachment to things as they are which every Soviet adult has learned simply by growing up in the country, that he was trying to overcome and that he was determined to overcome. Now, I was not surprised to hear the argument. At the time he had also said it in public, and it was a good, Gorbachevian point: intelligent, and politically useful, and perhaps even wise. Because what Soviet leaders say tends to be repeated, other Soviets were also saying it in public. But it was not true on its face, and I recalled it when I began to think about the end of the Cold War.

We hear much these days about the end of the Cold War, and it seems to me that Gorbachev's point applies by analogy to the Cold War too, and has the same basic character. Most of us carry the Cold War around with us, just as

4

individual Soviets carry the status quo around with them. It is part of the air we breathe. It is part of the way things are. It is part of the way we are. It is part of what must be overcome if we are to fashion a better world, for ourselves and our children. And it is intelligent, and politically useful, and perhaps even wise, to say so and to make going beyond the Cold War a political objective for ourselves and the rest of the world.

The trouble is that saying so and setting such an objective only take you so far. Gorbachev's argument that opposition to change is inside every Soviet, but only there, does not prove that there is no organized political opposition to reform in Soviet politics. In just the same way, saying that the Cold War is over does not prove it is over. And saying that it lives in each of us and must be overcome does not tell us how to end it.

It seems to me that this is true both in general and in each particular. To take only the largest, the most deeply rooted, the most intricately ramified component of the Cold War, it is a step in the right direction to say, as we and our allies say, and as the Soviets now say, that we must focus most particularly on ending the division of Europe. It is true to say that the Cold War began with that division and that the division of Europe in turn has perpetuated the Cold War. It is useful for political elites to set themselves the objective of effecting the kinds of change that will make whatever formally remains of that division irrelevant. Stating the goal is a big step. It is a step that is hard to take and important to take. But simply stating the goal takes you only a little way.

And the analogy extends beyond that. Gorbachev himself has discovered that change in the Soviet Union requires more than an impulse. It also requires a program. It requires defining goals and mobilizing political support for movement toward those goals that can be sustained over time. Slowly, painfully, and so far successfully, Gorbachev and his reform-minded colleagues in the leadership have developed such a program and gained and maintained and extended such support. But that political effort, or in other words politics, is the proper context for understanding Gorbachev's argument that opposition is in each of us but nowhere in particular. In that context the argument is just that, a political one, more or less true and more or less useful. And I think the same is true of the Cold War or the division of Europe. If we are interested in actually ending them, it is important and useful to agree on that objective, but more will be required. We will also need political programs, and these will involve millions of men and women, working through the issues and working out the issues in political terms over time. There is no escape from policy or from politics.

Once you enter the realm of politics, however, you enter the realm of controversy, of argument, of contention. This is precisely because millions of men and women are involved. They are more or less well represented by their leaders. They come at issues from different angles. They have different prejudices and passions and interests, which are more or less conscious, more or less politically articulated, more or less deeply held. And these must all be aggregated somehow by political systems and processes if there is to be movement in any direction at all. In that context, even the statement that the Cold War is over is contentious, because every statement on issues this important to public policy is contentious. Simply saying it is over arouses fears and resistance as well as hopes and efforts to move forward. And the tension among these various impulses can be resolved, or simply managed, only if it is handled in concrete political terms.

In this book I will be sharing some thoughts on the actual record of how these issues were in fact handled over the past decade. In the first four chapters, I will deal primarily with relations between the superpowers. In the next two I will treat the evolution of the division of Europe, the granddaddy of Cold War issue clusters. I have been a participant and a close observer of many of the events that constitute this record. I worked on the American side, so the point of view will necessarily be American. Also, I am not a leader, so what follows is very much a bricklayer's song. With these caveats, I should also say that I have tried to put together a record of these important and highly charged developments that is as accurate and as dispassionate I can make it. As Hobbes said, liberty is in the silence of the passions, and after eight passionate years that kind of record can at least be my objective.

Even a bricklayer needs benchmarks, and by way of opening I would like to offer a very few conceptual pointers. Everyone who works in the policy business explains policy so often in terms of such pointers that he or she ends up sounding Chinese. The Chinese enunciate policy in terms of four modernizations, three obstacles, and the like. Our Soviet policy in the 1980s developed three principles and a four-part agenda, but I will introduce them at their proper place in the narrative. What I have in mind here as introductory pointers are two traits and one major gap that characterized the United States and the Soviet Union a decade ago, as the 1970s drew to a close.

The first trait involves qualities the superpowers share but that pit them against each other. Both the U.S. and the USSR are huge countries, almost continents. Both are rich in natural resources, in the sinews of power in modern conditions. Both have large, diverse populations with relatively high educational levels. Historically, both have been outsiders or latecomers in international politics. This has given them an Avis mentality, which may be typical of new players, but which is certainly irritating to the others, particularly because these two are so powerful. Most of all, both the U.S. and the Soviet Union have carried forward from their origins as organized political systems a messianic approach to their role in the world. Both have a sense that they are somehow exceptional, that they are not subject to the rules that apply to others, or at least to all of them. On the contrary, both sense that they are endowed with some special mission to help mankind as a whole, to move human history forward. American and Soviet messianisms may not be appealing, especially to others, but they are a fact of international life. Criticizing them or wishing they would go away does no good. They have to be dealt with.

The importance of these divisive shared characteristics should not be exaggerated but often is. They are often cited to suggest that differences between the superpowers are so deep-rooted in history or in nature or in both, or in ideology expressing both, that they cannot be dealt with by political means. America's most distinguished diplomat-observer, George Kennan, has given wide currency to one variant of this view, which is that some issues, like nuclear war, can and must be managed through negotiation, but that others cannot be dealt with by political interaction because they reflect systemic differences rooted in history. In this view it follows that we should not even put Soviet human rights behavior on the negotiating table.

My view is that no differences are *that* deep-rooted. Not only must U.S.-Soviet differences be managed by political means in the nuclear age, but they *can* be. They must be managed prudently, carefully, and realistically. They must be managed without excessive expectations of positive change however defined. They cannot all be resolved at once. All that is true. But the questions of which issues to take up, which to press, and which *not* to press, are questions of policy and judgment rather than history. They are questions of choice.

Still, it is important not to forget the large differences that our shared qualities create. Soviets and Americans define their special missions differently, and that has been a large contributing factor to the Cold War. The political definitions of the missions can change over time, so that it is possible to narrow the differences as well as to expand them. Something of the sort may be going on now, as the Soviet leadership makes "all-human values" an objective of Soviet foreign policy that is somehow higher than class struggle. But even if the American and Soviet bodies politic narrow the differences in the way we define our special missions as much as possible, those missions will still be unique, and therefore different and competitive.

The second trait characterizing the superpower relationship a decade ago involved a contrast between U.S. and Soviet national approaches to domestic politics and foreign policy.

By this I do not mean our American national belief that democratic countries are necessarily more peaceful and cooperative in their foreign relations than others. That belief helps account for the current popularity of the notion that Gorbachev needs a breathing space in international affairs in order to concentrate Soviet energies on domestic reform. It may also explain some of the current attraction of the analogous notion that American foreign relations are in such good shape as the 1990s approach that we can now afford to turn to our deteriorating infrastructure — crime, drugs, schools, roads and bridges, competitiveness — after two generations of strenuous international exertion.

All these notions may reflect a real reality, in whole or in part, and I am not contesting them. There may be something to them. But their theoretical underpinning is shaky. I see no *necessary* connection between domestic and foreign policy approaches. We ourselves have a rich tradition of Cold War liberals, and I see nothing in Soviet experience that precludes such a phenomenon there, even one called Mikhail Gorbachev. Combining domestic reform with a more muscular foreign policy would be costly to Gorbachev, even very costly. But there are always costs in politics; politics is about balances of costs and benefits. What I have in mind is something else.

That is the contrast between the different ways the Soviet and American traditions deal with domestic and foreign policies, respectively. Historically the Russians and then the Soviets have sought to abolish domestic politics, the clash of interests and ideas with indeterminate outcomes that is the essence of politics for Westerners. They inhabit a part of the world where society is weak and the state very strong, and where the state has traditionally tried to impose societal uniformity and solidarity for some higher purpose and to mobilize usable power to help achieve it. That is in domestic politics. In foreign affairs, by contrast, the Russians and then the Soviets have often set grandiose long-term goals for themselves, but they have characteristically set rather modest objectives for the short and medium terms. These they have pursued patiently and with great determination, but at the same time they have usually also shown great respect for the realities of the outside environment.

We Americans have had precisely the converse approach. We have played the long game in domestic politics. The clash of interests and ideas, and agreed mechanisms for conducting it, are the core of our system. When we fought it was because the system broke down, and we imagined that the solution was to restore it. With us the state is weak, because that is the kind of state a strong society has wanted. When we repress, the state is often the handmaiden of society, sometimes its guide in eliminating repression, rarely its instigator. We believe in the open future with indeterminate outcomes.

But in foreign affairs, beyond the water's edge where domestic politics was supposed to stop, we Americans have traditionally sought the same kind of quick, total solutions that the Russians and Soviets have tried throughout their history to impose on their domestic scene. In foreign affairs we have been inclined to rapid mobilization of energies and extraordinary, strenuous effort aimed at establishing or reestablishing some nirvana, an end to struggle, that would permit us to return to our more congenial and more profitable domestic pursuits.

By the late 1970s those two traits — shared but divisive qualities and contrasting ways of handling domestic and foreign affairs — had consistently marked the conduct of the superpowers for the thirty years of the Cold War. But meanwhile what I would call a political phasing gap was opening up.

The Soviet Union was into its second decade of what is now, under the Gorbachev leadership, called stagnation. When Nikita Khrushchev was ousted in late 1964, the Soviet elite could look back on fifty years of almost unrelieved turbulence: war, then revolution, then civil war, then industrialization and collectivization, then the purges, then an even bigger, bloodier war, followed by more repression, and then Khrushchev's experimentation. Through a whole half century, politics had been a hard, all-or-nothing activity. It had intimately affected the lives of everyone in the country, and it had ended or ruined millions of those lives. Leonid Brezhnev's stabilization, including its famous cadre stability, meant that many things were badly done, but it also meant that people were increasingly left alone and allowed to develop some private life. When it was new and for many years thereafter, this was a precious, positive political benefit, and it was widely appreciated. But by the late 1970s it had gone on, and on, and on. It had become, precisely, an era, and the benefits were wearing thinner and thinner.

By the late 1970s the view was spreading in the Soviet elite itself that something was terribly wrong with the way things were going for the country and that something needed to be done. By the late Brezhnev years, more and more members of the elite were realizing that they were facing structural difficulties and not just mistakes that could be blamed on individuals or small groups in the traditional manner. They were coming to recognize that major change was required; that no one really knew what kind of change that meant; but that effecting it would be complex, difficult, and prolonged. In other words, there was a growing sense that a general crisis was brewing but that no quick or total fixes were available.

That was not, of course, what was said. It was something you had to deduce from the way the Soviets expressed their habitual confidence that things were all right, from tonalities, from their actions. Brezhnev was ill, and his colleagues in the leadership were old and getting older. This meant that their departure would bring not just new individuals but a whole new generation of political leaders to the fore. In the Soviet system personal relations are much more important even than in ours, and disorder is more feared because there has been so much of it. After three score years in power, the Soviet leadership still had the psychology of a guerrilla government, and the prospect of generational change reinforced its natural penchant to hang together in order not to hang separately. There was thus a tremendous premium on continuity in personnel, in policy, and in ideology, a premium on standing pat. What the Soviets actually did in the late 1970s was to insist that there was no alternative to the status quo and to circle the wagons against the outside world. In foreign affairs the USSR continued to do whatever it had been doing up to then, under the old ideological banners. This certainly included picking up targets of opportunity to extend Soviet influence in the Third World. But the Soviets became incapable of real novelty, and they found it harder and harder to respond creatively to novel situations. In one area after another contacts with the outside world that were considered threatening or illegitimate were geared down and cut off. To the extent it had been permitted before, emigration was throttled back. The dissident movement was eaten away by police action. Later on direct-dial telephoning was practically eliminated, and receipt of package mail became prohibitively difficult. These are just examples of a general trend. And meanwhile the economy ground down. Together, these developments sapped the faith of whole decades that all the sacrifices and shortages — of which Soviet citizens are well aware — actually had a larger purpose, that they actually served some long-term goal of social justice at home and a more peaceful and better world. In other words, the cost of stability was rising.

14

Meanwhile, we Americans were getting tired of instability. We were in our second decade of it. The presidential election campaign of 1960 had marked the peaceful transition to leadership by the new political generation that had come of age during and after World War II. But it also introduced years of unrelieved turmoil. The period is just coming up for serious scholarly analysis, not to speak of serious books and movies, as those who were young in it pass thirty and forty. The 1950s may have felt dull while they were going on, but by the late 1970s, after the civil rights struggle, after Vietnam, after Watergate, after the oil shocks, they were starting to look good again. America was getting ready for some peace and quiet.

That was not, of course, what was said. What we were telling ourselves was that we needed creative leadership to lead the country out of its confusion and into a brighter future, to tackle the problems it faced at home with greater energy and acumen, and to restore its position in the world. As is usual in our politics, the emerging national longing for stabilization was framed in terms of exciting advance. And as it turned out, that was not a bad thing.

For the first generation of the Cold War, from roughly the late 1940s until the 1960s, there had been a political consensus in this country about the approach we should take to dealing with the Soviet Union. Not only was there agreement that the Soviet Union was our major foreign policy problem, there was consensus in general terms on what to do about it. That was containment. Containment meant doing what we could to keep Soviet power and influence to the limits that the USSR had achieved in the early postwar period. This was to be done through systematic confrontation by all means short of military means. Almost everyone recognized that seeking military confrontation with the Soviets was not acceptable American policy in the nuclear age. But other than that, as the saying went, "anything goes."

That consensus for containment through systematic confrontation began to erode away in the 1960s. There were many reasons. The new political generation with its new, more contentious political habits had something to do with it. Vietnam — the revolt of their children, and the turning away from government in general — had something to do with it. And the relentless Soviet military buildup after the Cuban missile crisis of 1962, especially in strategic nuclear weapons, had a lot to do with it. So long as the United States enjoyed clearly perceived strategic superiority, systematic confrontation of the Soviets by non-military means was politically plausible because it was so unlikely to lead to military confrontation. Once the Soviets began to match us in many categories of strategic arms and to overshoot us in some, that plausibility eroded away, because even non-military confrontation was so much more likely to lead to military conflict. And when that plausibility went, so did consensus support for the policy approach.

The late 1960s and early 1970s saw an attempt to fashion a new consensus for Soviet policy to replace the one for containment that was disappearing. This attempt came to be called détente. From the beginning there was an ambiguity in the way it was defined politically. On the one hand, it was most often described as an effort to supplement containment's systematic confrontation with systematic negotiation. On the other hand, it was also described as an effort to move from an era of confrontation to an era of negotiation, as President Richard Nixon did in his first Inaugural Address in 1969. In the first case, negotiation was to be an add-on to confrontation, in the second, a substitute for it.

This ambiguity was perhaps politically necessary and even useful in the beginning, because in our politics a policy needs the support of a broad spectrum of constituencies. But as negotiations with the Soviets got underway in earnest in the early 1970s, the Administration began to justify them more and more in terms of creating "a new structure of peace," something basically different from the previous state. Many Americans who were willing to accept negotiations as a supplement to confrontation were unwilling to accept them as an alternative to it, in the old containment sense. And here they sensed a deeper real ambiguity in the Administration's approach.

Some of détente's authors were at heart convinced that it was simply the best available American policy for a time when historic trends were very unfavorable to the United States. It seemed to them that the Soviet Union might be barbaric, and irresponsible, and even dangerous, but that it was also a young, powerful country on a historic upward trend. By contrast, it seemed to them, the United States was embarked on a decline, at least in relative terms, probably also in absolute terms, however much it had preserved of its postwar preeminence. That was not the way they wanted it, but they believed that was the situation they faced. And they believed it was their responsibility as statesmen to recognize it and act on it.

Now, this was a plausible view at a time when it was impossible to get adequate defense budgets out of the U.S. Congress; when the political system, including the Congress, seemed determined to multiply restrictions on the decision-making authority of the so-called Imperial Presidency; and when political contest was bitter almost across the range of issues. But to act responsibly on this view meant trying to fix the point on the graph of history where the Soviet and American trends crossed, and to fix it by wit, by diplomacy, by negotiation, rather than by strength — for strength was not available.

Moreover, for negotiation to succeed it must reflect the interests of all the negotiating parties, and in the late 1960s and early 1970s when détente negotiations with the Soviets were engaged, practically the only common interest that the elites of the two countries could identify and accept unambiguously after a generation of Cold War contention was reducing the risk of nuclear war. Thus it happened that the détente agenda — the actual subject matter of government-to-government dialogue between the two countries in the 1970s — focused overwhelmingly on nuclear arms negotiations. There were also negotiations on some other arms issues, particularly during the Carter Administration. There were some economic relations, to which Congress added emigration via the Jackson-Vanik Amendment in late 1974, thereby introducing human rights, against the will of both the Soviets and the U.S. Administration. Finally, there was a modicum of respect, a kind of joint commitment to deal with each other soberly and fairly. This produced an impressive series of cooperative agreements in the scientific, cultural, and economic fields; it was codified in a number of impressive theoretical documents, statements of principles of various kinds; and it was justified as building a web of vested interests between the elites that in time of crisis would reduce the temptation to act in a hostile or belligerent fashion.

There were real achievements under this agenda. Many specific agreements have stood the test of a very hard time. Interaction among the elites did not prevent that hard time, but it produced a degree of mutual familiarity and even knowledge that made it impossible to return to the depths of ignorance and misapprehension which prevailed before détente. Nevertheless, the détente agenda was in fact very narrow. It left out very many of the contentious and divisive issues between the two superpowers that had accumulated over decades. In particular, it substantially omitted what came to be called regional issues, the third-area hotspots where both Soviet and American interests were engaged. And it left out systemic differences almost entirely. The two governments, of course, talked about such issues, sometimes frequently. They even negotiated on them, as in the negotiations in the Conference on Security and Cooperation in Europe (CSCE) that culminated in the Helsinki Final Act of 1975 and continued thereafter. But regional issues and systemic differences were not among the "core" or "central" issues that by common consent dominated the détente agenda. And when the two countries came into conflict, the statements of principles they had negotiated became apples of discord, because these statements necessarily papered over differences of interpretation. When either side appealed to them, it simply made the other madder.

Détente failed to capture consensus support in American politics. The actual history of its failure, under three administrations — two Republican and one Democratic — is complex and still controversial. As with the erosion of containment, there were a variety of reasons. The accelerated disaffection with government symbolized by the words Vietnam and Watergate had something to do with it. A familiar pattern of Soviet secrecy had something to do with it. With the completion of a major arms modernization effort that left the USSR in very good shape compared to us, Soviet military procurement leveled off after mid-decade, but because the Soviets conceal military secrets we did not discern this until 1983. What we saw instead was relentless buildup, turning the military balance against the United States in category after category. And a new pattern of Soviet behavior in the Third World had a lot to do with it. Although the Soviets are generally more skeptical about American statements on our weakness than we are, it seems to me fair to say that over the course of the decade they began to take what they heard from us about our weakness more seriously and to seize opportunities for promoting and extending their influence in the Third World with more agility, and especially with more military force.

The reasons for this new behavior are still debated. I have heard it argued that they were merely imitating us, learning old lessons about military power and political influence monkey-see monkey-do, just at the moment when we were unlearning some of them. I suspect that they also turned more to power projection via military means partly through subtraction. With their own economic difficulties, it was getting harder for them to generate economic aid, and Soviet ideology was becoming less attractive in the Third World as decolonization proceeded and they became stodgier at home. But whatever the reasons, the pattern of behavior itself does not seem to me debatable. In the 1970s the Soviets came to rely more and more on military means to compete in third areas. They fielded a blue-water navy and became a global power at last. They used their newly accrued military resources to promote their influence in an expanding list of third-area conflict situations. They were also successful. The list of countries "falling" to political forces friendly to and in important ways dependent on the Soviets — what can be called the Solzhenitsyn list — grew and grew and grew. It is worth recalling: Vietnam in early 1975; the introduction of Cuban forces into the Angolan civil war in late 1975; South Yemen and Ethiopia in 1977 and 1978; the Vietnamese invasion of Cambodia in 1978; then the Soviet invasion of Afghanistan in 1979; and after the Sandinista victory in Nicaragua that same year, the guerrilla "Final Offensive" in El Salvador during the transition from Carter to Reagan.

The strength of the Reagan offensive against President Ford for the Republican nomination in 1976 had already destroyed any near-term prospect for a SALT II Treaty on strategic nuclear arms. It had even backed the Ford administration off further use of the very word détente. Before there was an L-word, there was a D-word. But it was four more years before Ronald Reagan was to be inaugurated as President, and the Carter years were also eventful. As it happened, they were not just eventful in terms of détente's agony. As we can now see, they also laid the basis for what has come after.

The turning point came in 1978. When it looked out in the spring of that year at the prospect of the fall congressional elections, the Carter Administration came to an important political conclusion. It saw, or more accurately felt, that the American electorate rather liked the rich menu of U.S.-Soviet arms-control negotiations then underway, from SALT through nuclear test ban and Mutual and Balanced Force Reduction (MBFR) talks all the way down to the Indian Ocean and conventional arms transfers. The electorate rather liked the new stress the Administration was putting, this time of its own free will, on Soviet human rights behavior. But what the electorate was worried about, what defined the American Soviet policy as a political issue, was weakness. What the electorate cared most about, and did not like, was the Administration's perceived inability to cope with the Soviet Union, to muster the requisite strength and savvy to deal with the Soviet threat.

This concern for strength and weakness struck in two directions in American politics. It meant first of all that the American people had sniffed out the secret sense of détente's authors that the United States was somehow in historical decline vis-à-vis the Soviet Union, and found it unacceptable. Second, it meant that the electorate did not

22

take kindly either to the deep divisions within the government over what the U.S. approach to the Soviet Union should be — divisions that were symbolized by the feuding between Secretary of State Cyrus Vance and National Security Advisor Zbigniew Brzezinski — or to their President's claim that there was little if anything government as such could do about the problem, or other problems of public policy either. The electorate was having none of it, either the weakness or the lack of jurisdiction.

The Administration's first response was to propose more defense spending. So it was in that year, 1978, under Carter — rather than in 1981 or 1982, under Reagan — that U.S. defense spending in real terms began to rise again for the first time in almost a decade. But there were significant developments in 1979 as well. This was the year of the debate over ratification of the SALT II Treaty finally signed by Carter and Brezhnev that summer in Vienna. It was, in fact, a debate over how the United States should handle the Soviet Union. More than most American political debates, it was not only animated but also intelligent and thorough. And unlike most, it even had a political conclusion.

The conclusion was that the American electorate wanted something new in its government's approach to the other superpower. What emerged from the SALT II debate was the makings of a new political consensus. What the electorate wanted from its government in dealing with the Soviet Union was not strength alone — the systematic confrontation of the containment consensus — or negotiations alone — negotiations as an alternative to strength. Instead, it wanted strength and negotiations together, in tight combination, reinforcing each other. It wanted the original détente promise that détente policy had failed to keep.

And this was something new under the sun in terms of the traditional American approach to adversaries. We do not treat either our friends or ourselves that way, but with regard to adversaries we have traditionally sought the victorious "quick fix" that will solve all our problems. When we were strong, it made no sense to negotiate; unconditional surrender was the American paradigm for dealing with such problems. And if we negotiated it somehow meant that we were weak; that was the brush that tarred détente. Now, instead of either, we insisted on both together.

Another set of developments in 1979 produced yet another important political result. Because the SALT II debate was so focused on nuclear arms control, it was not so visible as the emerging consensus for strength and negotiation together, but it was visible nonetheless. It had to do with the composition and shape of the U.S.-Soviet agenda. The Carter Administration tried to keep the SALT II ratification process alive regardless of deteriorating Soviet human rights performance and accelerating Soviet activism against our interests in third-area situations. This reflected the traditional elite view that nuclear arms control was the central issue, preeminent over all others. The Administration's decision to withdraw the treaty from Senate consideration in the wake of the Soviet invasion of Afghanistan in December showed beyond any doubt that this view could no longer be politically sustained. The lesson was that an arms-control-centered agenda was too narrow to keep even arms control alive.

This experience showed that while most Americans feel most of the time that there is a Soviet threat, the actual political definition of where the Soviets are most threatening changes over time. Sometimes it is Soviet arms — the question of the military balance. Sometimes it is how those arms are used — Soviet expansionism in third areas. Sometimes it is why the Soviet Union is expansionist — the question of the Soviet system, how it treats its own people and is thus likely to treat foreigners and foreign countries. And the lesson was that the U.S.-Soviet agenda must be comprehensive, that it must cover all the significant issues between the two countries, the hard and divisive issues as well as those that are more promising. The U.S.-Soviet agenda must give every significant sector of American political opinion the assurance that its issue will not be neglected or traded off in the negotiating end game of some other issue. In other words, only a comprehensive U.S.-Soviet agenda can be sustained in American politics.

These lessons came too late for the Carter Administration. President Carter did not, of course, lose the 1980 election to President Reagan merely because he was a slow learner about Soviet policy. As in most U.S. presidential elections, foreign policy was not the main issue then. The main issue was overall competence, and on that score Soviet policy was only one item on a general and rather extensive bill of indictment. But it is worth setting out this old chronology ten years later, because it shows that the makings of the new consensus on our Soviet policy antedated the Reagan Administration. Out there in public opinion there was support for both strength and negotiation; there was the insistence that government treat them not as alternatives to one another, but in tight harness; and there was the requirement that all the issues, the good, the bad, and the ugly, be dealt with seriously by our Soviet policy. This was a mix that the Reagan Administration as political competitors helped to create and that it inherited with its landslide victory in 1980. Along with the new elements of consensus came the task of building it out into a policy approach. How it did so is the story of the next chapter.

Chapter 2

The Dynamics of American New Thinking: U.S.- Soviet Relations 1981-1983

The first two years of the Reagan Administration were a hard time in U.S.-Soviet relations and came before Gorbachev, so it is also the least well known and the least well understood part of the story of what happened during the decade. But it is an essential part.

In retrospect, we can see that developments in the late 1970s laid the groundwork for new departures in U.S.-Soviet relations by the time President Reagan came to office in January 1981. We can now see that the Soviet elite was gearing up to "get the country moving again," as we used to say about ourselves in the Kennedy years. We can see that we ourselves were in fact moving toward stabilization in politics and society after twenty years of turmoil. But at the time the outlook was very uncertain. The Soviet superpower had somehow become predictable in doing what it had been doing. It was perhaps dangerous, but it was no longer creative, and it had even become insufferably dull in its very predictability. When it came to the United States, it was perhaps true that we were heading toward a new stability, but if so we were certainly doing it in a tremendous public scrum and at very high decibel levels.

Still, the signs were there. The main sign was that the incoming Reagan Administration defined its mandate for change as a mandate to turn the country around, toward a better America that had existed sometime before. The Reagan Revolution was to be a restoration. As the President put it in his first Inaugural Address, we were to become once again "the city on the hill." Still, political systems often move forward in the name of going back to a golden age, and backing toward the future was at least movement. With the Soviet Union mired in the status quo, this meant it was up to the United States to set the pace and direction of U.S.-Soviet relations.

When it came to dealing with the Soviets the new Administration's approach was shaped by two impulses. In the first place, its own priorities were overwhelmingly domestic. The primary object of the restorative revolution was to be America itself rather than the world. So the initial priorities were, in order: to restore America's economic health; to achieve a substantial measure of rearmament; and when it came to foreign affairs proper, to restore America's alliances and friendships around the world, to stop penalizing our friends and start penalizing our enemies again, as the slogan went. In practical terms this meant that the Administration's Soviet policy was going to be a sort of residual of these other priorities. It implied that we would be ready to deal more capably than we had in the 1970s with what looked like a surging USSR only when the economy was in better shape and we had done some rearmament and had put our relations with allies and friends back on track.

Second, what we were mainly conscious of vis-à-vis the Soviets was our own weakness, so our approach was in fact highly defensive. The Soviets at the time saw their task as defending the gains of generations of effort. In relations with us that meant defending what they called "rough parity" in the military balance and "equality" in political relations, which they saw as the main fruits of détente in the 1970s. We saw things differently. We believed that they had overshot and that our task was to make up the shortfalls. We thought we were playing catch-up ball.

The emerging consensus on Soviet affairs in the country called for both strength and negotiation together. This was understood, and from the beginning there was no argument within the government that our policy had to include both. But because we were so impressed with our own weakness, there was also no real argument against concentrating first of all on rebuilding our strength and downplaying negotiations until we had restored enough strength to "negotiate from strength." The real argument had to do not with the sequence — first strength, then negotiation — but with timing — how fast we should move into negotiation. There were very many in those early days who feared a quick return to the slippery slope back to détente, and they were perfectly happy to see the structure of the slope dismantled and negotiations put off as long as possible. Those who were more confident that America

31

was strong enough and smart enough to deal sensibly with the Soviet challenge wanted to keep most of the inherited structure of relations in place, as a framework for renewed negotiations when the time came, and to shorten the delay. They therefore tended to argue at any given point that we had *already* recovered our strength and confidence sufficiently to get negotiations going again.

Most of this argument was in fact not about Russia. It was really about America, about whether we had the capacity and will to defend our national interests in relations with the USSR. This was true even — or especially — when the argument took the form of competing analyses of what the Soviets were and what they wanted. And an argument that is basically about America cannot be resolved immediately in terms of policy. So in those early years the policy device that filled the middle ground between restorative buildup and negotiating decisions that could not yet be taken was rhetoric.

Moreover, this rhetoric was more than just a political device, and more than just a way to restore American confidence without actually confronting the Soviets. It also reflected President Reagan's own conception of leadership. It will be some time before we have a satisfactory explanation of this mysterious man and President. But it already seems to me possible to say that his own concept of what he should be doing as a leader called on him largely to express values that most Americans shared, as persuasively as possible but above all firmly and consistently. His job was to say true things and keep saying them. And given his own experience with and views on Communists, given the very real ideological differences between the two super-powers, and given the recent record of Soviet conduct, in those early years the rhetoric about the Soviet Union that accompanied his American restoration, and in his concept contributed to it, was very harsh indeed.

This in turn was a real problem for the Soviets and many Europeans. By its nature the rhetoric left open all the questions about what to do, and in the meantime it was very anti-Soviet. What the Soviets and many West Europeans heard in it was aggressive intent, a poisoning of the atmosphere that had to be intentional. The rhetoric sounded as if it were positively designed to support an arms buildup that would restore lost American military superiority, or at least force the Soviets into another, frightfully expensive round of the arms race that would "bring them to their knees" economically. The fact that there were people in our big government who talked that way, including occasionally the President himself, did not help.

During the 1970s the Soviets had espoused the theory that the historic "correlation of forces" was shifting in favor of socialism, meaning themselves, and that détente meant American acceptance of this fact. In the early 1980s they were still impaled on that theory. They felt they had been playing catch-up ball for over six decades. In their own eyes, they had just caught up, and just barely at that. They therefore interpreted any American advance as breaking parity and reestablishing superiority. Our new objective of "negotiating from strength" sounded to them like intimidation or, as they put it, "dictation." In other words, we thought we were playing catch-up ball, to reestablish a balance they had disturbed, and what they thought they were hearing was American determination to break out of parity and equality, back to the American superiority that they insisted we had finally agreed to put behind us in the 1970s.

And in those early years there were no real negotiations underway to provide actual tests of American and Soviet intentions. So the Soviets had the traditional reaction of their state since its foundation when it has been blocked in its direct dealings with other states. They responded with a propaganda campaign that went over, under, and around the Reagan Administration, to public opinion, to other states, to elements of their societies. Whatever else this propaganda was intended to achieve, they wanted it to build pressure on us to return to negotiations on an acceptable basis. They were fortified by self-righteous hurt feelings, just as we were. But they were also locked in by their attachment to whatever they had previously been doing and saying, as we most emphatically were not. So when they turned to Europe, to Western public opinion, and to American society to pressure us, they fixed on the nuclear issue. The accusation was that the Reagan Administration was tearing everything down in order to prepare for what must inevitably be nuclear war.

But for the Soviets to accept the rhetorical challenge and identify the issue as the risk of nuclear war cut in contradictory directions in American politics. On the one hand, because it had some resonance in Western Europe, it drove two of the Administration's own priorities up against each other. We wanted *both* to restore America's military strength and to restore the health of our alliances. As long as there were many in the Western alliance who doubted our sincerity about negotiating with the Soviets, it was going to be much harder to restore our leadership and Western strength. To do that, we had to listen to our allies. But if we listened to our allies on arms control, we reinforced what I would call the Administration's vertical split between the elected leadership and the policy apparatus underneath.

For about the first year the Administration's anti-Soviet rhetoric was not much of a political problem in this country. The President and his colleagues liked to operate on that terrain, and to the others it seemed like a useful way to rebuild American self-confidence after the buffetings of the 1970s. The trouble was with the other half of the President's leadership concept. Within that concept, his job was to enunciate values that mobilized energy and made it available to move the country in the right directions. But actually turning that energy into policies that would work was someone else's job. The President recognized that he would be called on to arbitrate conflicting advice. But he was genial at putting off this task. The Reagan Administration had a broad consensus on the basics of Soviet policy at the cabinet level. Everyone agreed that the Soviet Union was this country's most important foreign policy problem; that it was a big, different, and potentially dangerous great power with which we would have to deal; and that to deal with it we would need strength, realism, and negotiations (or dialogue — it depended on the speaker). These Chinese-style three principles for U.S. Soviet policy were put in place early on. But there was no good way of translating cabinet consensus on these principles across the vertical divide between the cabinet level and the policy formulation level, and this guidance vacuum left the field open to high bureaucratic contest. It created the squabbling for which these years are famous, and it plunged policy into the realm of politics, of political and bureaucratic contingency.

Moreover, when the Soviets defined the problem largely in terms of the risk of nuclear war, they guaranteed that the American policy battle would continue to be fought on the old 1970s terrain. When détente began, reducing the risk of nuclear war had been practically the only common interest the elites of the two countries could identify, and strategic arms talks therefore dominated the détente agenda. The Soviet propaganda offensive meant that this continued to be the case in the early Reagan years. The Soviets, much of public opinion, and almost all the U.S. policy players in those years invested nuclear arms control with much larger hopes and fears. They made progress on nuclear arms or lack of it the test of how East-West relations were going and how the individual players were doing. So the struggle was intense. Good books have been written about it from the perspective of 1984 and 1985, the Administration's middle years. A distinguished example is Strobe Talbott's *Deadly Gambits*, whose very title expresses the point of view and the time, the concept of a game with mortal stakes. So I do not need to repeat a record that already exists. My theme is rather the hidden dynamics of how we transcended it.

It was recognized by all that nuclear arms negotiations would come, if only because domestic and West European opinion insisted on them. The struggle was therefore not between those who wished to engage them and those who did not. Rather, it was between those who wished to begin soon, with U.S. negotiating positions that were politically plausible, and those who wished to delay negotiations as long as possible and make them as difficult as possible once they started. Given the President's allergy to arbitration, this tension could be dealt with only issue by concrete issue. And the first issues that came up concerned intermediate-range nuclear forces in Europe, or INF.

The Administration had inherited the problem. In the mid-1970s the Soviets had begun to deploy new and vastly more threatening INF missiles, the SS-20's. The fact that they were targeted against NATO Europe and could not reach us raised concerns among our allies, and particularly the West Germans, that the new deployments would weaken the U.S. commitment to defend Western Europe, if necessary by putting the continental United States at strategic risk. In response to these concerns, in December 1979 the NATO countries took a difficult, dual-track decision concerning these INF weapons. On the first track, NATO decided that by late 1983 the U.S. would deploy in Europe a limited number of new American missiles, the Pershing II's and ground-launched cruise missiles or GLCMs. The second track would be U.S.-Soviet negotiations to solve the problem in the meantime. Politically, this meant that persuasive good-faith negotiations had to take place if deployments were to occur. The alternative to negotiation was a defeat for NATO, and by extension for two key Administration commitments, to rebuild our defenses and to rebuild our alliances.

This dilemma was unwelcome because it had been inherited from the Carter Administration, but it was also unavoidable. It was dealt with piecemeal in a series of ferocious bureaucratic battles that lasted through 1981 and that focused in the end on what our going-in position should be in the negotiations then scheduled to begin in November. The outcome was that the warring factions came together on the so-called zero option. On November 18 President Reagan called for total elimination of Soviet missiles in this range in return for no American deployments at all. Like the original concern over decoupling, the concept of the zero option originated in West Germany. But through this set of circumstances, it set a pattern of American practice that became typical in the aftermath.

The zero option became the first of a series of ambitious American objectives enunciated without much regard for their negotiability with the Soviets. The zero option was bold, it was simple, and it hogged the public high road. All these qualities pleased the President. The thought of eliminating nuclear weapons pleased him too, though that became clear only later. Just as important in terms of the vertical split between the cabinet and the policy formulation levels of American government, the zero option also pleased the tribes squabbling down below. For those who believed in arms control it provided a start. For those who did not believe in INF arms control but did believe that what was called "alliance management" was critical to getting our missiles deployed, it passed the European anti-nuclear left on its left. And for those who believed arms control was a slippery slope back to détente, a "soporific" that prevented America from doing what it should do to maintain its strength, as Defense Assistant Secretary Richard Perle once called it, it looked perfectly non-negotiable. Up to that point the Soviet Union had never negotiated away a major system it had already deployed, and it had a position which insisted on its right to as many INF missiles as all its neighbors combined, while denying our right to deploy a single one.

At the time, indeed, the zero option *was* non-negotiable. But if it ever *became* negotiable, it would be a solution good for the United States, good for its allies, and for those who cared about such things, good for the Soviet Union too. The Soviets did not believe it for a minute. Neither did those who saw negotiability — asking only for what the Soviets could stand to give up in any given negotiation — as the acid test of U.S. seriousness and sincerity. But setting what Richard Perle called "a high standard" without much regard to negotiability made a lot of sense in terms of political support for sound American Soviet policy. If we could identify bold, simple, ambitious objectives for negotiations, objectives that would serve our interest if achieved, and if such objectives were broadly understood and accepted by the American political class, they would be immune to the temptation of linkage.

Linkage was one of the most vexed and vexing issues inherited from the 1970s. The concept of linkage is to make American moves in areas of interest to the Soviets only in return for Soviet moves of interest to us, or to punish the Soviets in areas they care about for ugly, irresponsible, or dangerous behavior in areas we care about, whether or not the areas are related on their merits. It is a natural concept for Americans, because our domestic politics is so much a matter of compromise and trade-off. But it was ultra-natural for Americans in the 1970s, a decade when many of us felt that we were playing the Soviets with poor cards, perhaps against a stacked deck. So it was applied in a number of famous cases. In 1974 the Congress linked trade and Jewish emigration in the Jackson-Vanik Amendment. In 1980, after the Soviet invasion of Afghanistan, the Carter Administration had not only withdrawn the SALT II Treaty from Senate consideration, but had also embargoed grain exports to the Soviets, and boycotted the Moscow Olympics. Now, in the 1980s, the practice of setting bold objectives with high standards that would be to U.S. advantage if they were met made linkage much less natural. Short of a general crisis, it would not make sense to stop pursuing such objectives, to punish ourselves by depriving ourselves of a real potential benefit, simply in order to punish the Soviets. Linkage looked more and more like cutting off our nose to spite our face.

In the wake of the zero option, in any event, we proceeded to set such clear, demanding American objectives in area after area of U.S.-Soviet relations. And it was this process that made these years between 1981 and 1983 the years of American new thinking.

In arms control, we set ourselves the goal of deep, equitable, militarily significant, stabilizing, and verifiable reductions in weapons, rather than simply capping the arms race. In strategic arms negotiations, now rebaptized START, the INF situation reproduced itself, this time closer to home. Because the SS-20's threatened them and raised Transatlantic questions about Western deterrence, the West Europeans were transfixed by INF. By contrast, U.S. public opinion cared more about START, and when the peace movement came of age in this country in the spring of 1982 it focused on strategic arms and specifically on the nuclear freeze. The fall congressional elections were beginning to appear on political screens, and the freeze movement was eating into constituencies the Administration wanted to win, such as Catholics and Lutherans. As in INF, the response was a bold, simple proposal. In May 1982, at his own college in Eureka, Illinois, the President announced we would seek reductions of over 50 per cent in the Soviet land-based intercontinental ballistic missiles that threatened the land-based leg of our own strategic triad.

But the list of gripping goals was not confined to arms control. It extended to regional issues as well. We were having little success in putting them on the formal U.S.-Soviet agenda, and the Soviets were extremely wary of our efforts to do so. They had little to say about such issues themselves, and they wanted to keep the political focus on arms control. Consequently they were afraid the Administration would trumpet empty dialogue on non-arms-control issues as implying Soviet agreement to downgrade arms control. So here too we formulated big, ambitious objectives. In supporting Pakistan in the indirect talks on Afghanistan which were starting under United Nations sponsorship, we sought total Soviet withdrawal; reestablishment of Afghan independence and non-aligned status; a government that reflected the will of the Afghan people; and safe and honorable return of the millions of refugees outside the country. On that basis we would be willing to guarantee a political settlement together with the Soviet Union. For Cambodia, in support of ASEAN, our objective was total Vietnamese withdrawal. In southern Africa Assistant Secretary of State Chester Crocker was trying to broker a diplomatic solution requiring total withdrawal of all foreign forces from Angola and Namibia.

Nor was the list confined only to arms control and regional issues. At Westminster in June 1982 the President put the United States behind democracy, human rights, and fundamental freedoms and the rule of law everywhere in the world. It was a general commitment, for all peoples and not just those in Communist countries. But in the Soviet case it meant we were calling for radical improvements in human rights behavior and increases in Jewish emigration in particular. In our bilateral dealings with the Soviets, we introduced a whole new stress on the need for reciprocity and for a clear balance of advantages that would include advantage for us as well as them.

Much of the agenda thus defined became the substance of U.S.-Soviet relations in the late 1980s. But its emergence as our preferred agenda for bilateral dialogue was neither fast nor easy. The Soviets were not just wary; they were usually positively resistant. Their policy line was to restore everything that had been achieved in the 1970s and that the United States was breaking down. That was precisely what we did *not* have in mind: we were seeking something new and better.

Meanwhile, relations continued to bump downhill. It may be that martial law in Poland in December 1981 was better for the Poles and for us than the Soviet invasion we and our allies had prepared for. But at the time it looked to us like another Soviet-supported use of military force to impose a political solution against the popular will and our interests. It seemed very much in the pattern of Soviet behavior in third areas we had seen emerging in the 1970s. In response, the President lighted candles for the Poles and applied sanctions against the Polish government, but he also proceeded to impose another series of sanctions against the Soviets like those that had followed the Afghanistan invasion.

Because there were no real negotiations underway that would test the intentions of each side in concrete terms, each small issue in U.S.-Soviet relations took on cosmic policy significance in Washington. Each became a test case of U.S. resolve. We stood at Armageddon over whether to issue a visa. Civilization as we know it depended on whether or not to start talking to the Soviets about some eminently practical problem. And each debate was weighted in favor of getting tough, or at least doing nothing.

It took time, struggle, and special circumstances to get U.S. policy off dead center. The tension between rearmament and alliance management, combined with Soviet passivity, produced bold new proposals. These won us the high ground in the battle for public opinion, and this in turn strengthened Administration confidence. Meanwhile the continuing internal struggle over every step in arms control wore policymakers down. It was the combination and sequence of these factors that produced the new, broader U.S. agenda for dialogue with the Soviets. All over Washington, we began to stress that rebuilding our strength and rebuilding our alliances — the Administration's original priorities — were positively intended to create a new basis for productive dialogue with the Soviets, but that to be productive this dialogue would have to go beyond the old arms-control-centered agenda to include *all* the issues between the two countries, and especially regional issues and human rights.

Such were the makings of the new four-part U.S.-Soviet agenda: human rights, arms control, regional issues and bilateral issues. It had modest formal beginnings. During his year and a half in office, Secretary of State Alexander Haig gave top billing in his talks with Foreign Minister Andrei Gromyko to geopolitical issues — the regional issues of the later agenda — along with arms control. He did indeed raise bilateral issues and U.S.-interest human rights cases (divided families, divided spouses, and dual nationals), but by the end of his tenure in June 1982 we still defined our preferred agenda as "regional security, military security, human rights and other bilateral issues," in that order. Arms control was included in military security and human rights were still subsumed under bilateral issues. They became a separate agenda item only under Secretary of State George Shultz. Shultz recognized and shared President Reagan's conviction that one reason the Soviets were expansionist abroad was that they were not accountable at home. In that view, reliable domestic liberalization would be the best possible guarantee that the USSR was becoming a responsible participant in world affairs. So at the turn of 1982-1983, Shultz broke human rights out and gave them top billing, or what came to be called "pride of place," on the American agenda for dialogue.

Shultz was very gingerly in approaching the arms-control tarbaby, but he was lumbered immediately upon his entry into office with another fixture of the old détente agenda. That agenda had consisted of a lot of arms control, some economic relations, and a modicum of respect, with basically free competition elsewhere. By 1982 arms control was alive if not well, because the elites believed it was vital, and much of the American elite also continued to believe that economic relations were terribly important to the Soviets. Economic ties were therefore tempting targets when it came time to impose sanctions, and the sanctions we imposed after Afghanistan and after Polish martial law had been mainly economic. While Haig was meeting with Gromyko in New York in June 1982, the Administration in Washington announced new sanctions on exports of gas pipeline equipment to the USSR, and we made clear that we expected our European allies to follow suit. Haig had not been informed of the decision, and it helped trigger his resignation. So it was over to Shultz.

As with most other policy issues in this period, the argument over whether or not to cut off pipeline technology was mainly intra-Western; the Soviets were not much involved. The ostensible motive was to punish them for not letting up on Poland, but the real issue was larger. Like the argument over when we should proceed to negotiations with them, it had to do with how America and the West should handle the Soviet threat. Those who promoted economic sanctions tended to feel that the Soviet Union was so strong militarily that we could not possibly confront it until our own military rebuilding was at or near completion, but so weak economically that a small push would really hurt *its* military capacity. Economic sanctions were thus to be a surrogate for the military strength we did not or did not yet have. Those of us who were more confident about America's capacity to defend our interests vis-à-vis the Soviets with what we had already were more willing to see military force used and more skeptical about economic sanctions. But because the real argument was about America rather than about the Soviet Union, it could not be resolved politically as a matter of principle. It could be resolved only on a case-by-case basis, under the pressure of events.

So it was with the gas pipeline sanctions. Here, as in INF, the pressure came from our West European allies. In January 1982, after martial law was proclaimed in Poland, they had agreed to impose sanctions, but only as long as the sanctions could be reversed once the Poles met certain conditions. Now, six months later, we were back asking them to join the new cutoff of pipeline technology on the grounds that none of the conditions had yet been met. But what they remembered was that the President had lifted Carter's grain embargo against the Soviets to fulfill a campaign promise. It looked to them as if we were trying to limit their economic ties with the Soviets, which were mainly in manufacturing, while most of ours, which were in agriculture, were to be left intact. That looked like American self-interest rather than American leadership, and they bridled. And meanwhile alliance unity was still essential if INF deployments were to go forward by late 1983. Shultz spent much of his first year developing a diplomatic solution to this imbroglio, and it was consummated only at the Williamsburg Economic Summit in mid-1983.

Thus the old détente agenda was still an obstacle to the new, broader agenda of the 1980s. And yet, in that summer of 1982 there were also signs that some of the earlier passions were cooling.

First, INF negotiator Paul Nitze survived his famous July "Walk in the Woods." Together with his Soviet counterpart, but with little or no cover from Washington, he worked out a compromise concept for an early INF agreement. It was disavowed by both governments, but Nitze was nevertheless not fired, and in fact he went on to contribute to the Administration's later achievements. A year earlier he would have been out.

Second, we conducted a remarkably non-contentious overall review of our Soviet policy that summer and fall. It concluded sensibly that the U.S. should have three broad objectives in dealing with the Soviets. First, we should seek to contain and if possible reverse Soviet expansion. Second, we should use the limited means at our disposal to encourage movement toward greater pluralism and democracy in the Soviet Union. Third, we should negotiate agreements with the Soviets that would be in the U.S. national interest. The first objective, containing Soviet expansionism, had been the traditional goal of the containment consensus. The third, seeking good agreements, had been an integral part of policy since the 1960s. The second, encouraging internal change, sounded more portentous, because it resurrected an Eisenhower Administration goal. But it fit well within the worldwide democracy program, and recognizing that our means were limited defined it with a modesty suitable for dealing with another superpower.

Third and finally, that summer we also considered what we should do in the increasingly plausible contingency of Brezhnev's death, and the debate and conclusion were similarly non-contentious. All agreed that we should send Vice President Bush to the funeral with a message of policy continuity and constructive intent. And when Brezhnev died in November and was replaced by ex-KGB chief Yuriy Andropov, that was also the guidance that was followed. It was the first funeral of a sitting General Secretary since Stalin's in 1953, and the Soviets were mobilized both for the street turbulence that accompanied Stalin's death and for hostile pressure from the outside world. Moscow was like an armed Disney set run by the KGB. Andropov was conciliatory, and I suspect the Soviets were relieved at our basically conciliatory reaction. But 1983 was clearly going to be a critical year.

And so it was. It seems clear to me that 1983 rather than 1985 or 1986 was the real turning point in U.S.-Soviet relations during this decade. But it did not just happen, and it is worth describing the contingent ways in which the turn was made.

It was not made either through summitry or through arms control. Summit talk had died out in 1982 as Brezhnev entered his terminal decline, and when it picked up again under Andropov in early 1983, it still did not seem very real. START was simply deadlocked. Both sides continued to adjust their INF positions, but that was just part of the "battle for Europe." So the turn came through the service entrance, via the odds and sods of the relationship.

At that point in relations with the United States, the new Soviet leadership was talking simply about ways of conducting dialogue rather than about substance. So in January 1983, when Secretary Shultz suggested to Soviet Ambassador Anatoliy Dobrynin that they conduct a thorough review of bilateral relations and issues, Dobrynin quickly accepted. When they met on February 15 Shultz spirited Dobrynin off and took him up the White House back stairs for Ronald Reagan's first encounter with a senior Soviet. The talk lasted well over an hour. The President spent some time on overall relations, the causes of mistrust; some on arms control, where he showed he knew the issues; and about a third on human rights, and especially the case of the Soviet Pentecostalist families confined in our Moscow Embassy since 1978. It was the kind of human case that stirred his imagination and had symbolic political significance for him. And he told Dobrynin that such cases ought generally to be resolved quietly, without crowing.

After the meeting with the President, Shultz and Dobrynin went through bilateral issues in good spirits. Both conversations had results.

The first came less than two weeks later, in a Soviet message saying they would handle the Pentecostalist case "taking all factors into account." It was a very slight shift in position, but we chose to interpret it as positive. We responded positively, and the case began to move. The details are complex, but by April the families had left our embassy. In the meantime, in March, the President had described the Soviet Union to a group of evangelicals in Orlando as "the focus of evil" in the modern world. That same month he unveiled his strategic defense initiative, his proposal to see if a defense against incoming ballistic missiles could be developed that would make nuclear weapons "impotent and obsolete." So he was clearly not changing his views on the basics. On the contrary, from the Soviet point of view he was reinforcing them and adding worrisome new strings to his bow. But in the case of the Moscow Pentecostals, the Soviets were at least willing to test his sincerity about not crowing over human rights. And as the releases proceeded, we did handle them about as quietly as an American government can.

Then, in April and May, Secretary Shultz decided to move a number of small, deadlocked bilateral issues through the thicket of the bureaucracy. On two of them — negotiating a new exchanges agreement and going forward to open new American and Soviet consulates in Kiev and New York — he went directly to the President, and got his authorization to proceed.

Meanwhile Senate Foreign Relations Committee hearings on U.S.-Soviet relations which had been scheduled for the spring were deferred until June 15 because of Shultz's preoccupation with the Middle East. The timing thus had no political significance, and the testimony prepared for Shultz was also perfectly flat, a straight exposition of the U.S. approach without political signals of any kind. The trouble was that the two main papers Washingtonians read interpreted the testimony in diametrically opposed ways. In *The New York Times* Phil Taubman picked out the positive portions and announced that Shultz had struck a new, constructive note. In *The Washington Post* Don Oberdorfer picked out the harsher passages and announced that Shultz had unveiled a harder line. The bureaucracy was forced to choose between them in order to brief on what the Secretary had actually meant.

And official Washington decided that the answer was that we were doing pretty well vis-à-vis the Soviet Union. Looking back on the Administration's original priorities, we could observe that economic recovery was underway; that we had achieved a substantial measure of rearmament; and that after the Williamsburg Summit and resolution of the gas pipeline controversy, our relations with friends and allies were pretty good. In other words, the Administration had set priorities and made real progress toward them. Paradoxically, it had come to power running against government, and now two years later it was making government work. And when it came to U.S.-Soviet relations, which had been the residual of the other priorities, we had now told ourselves and the world so often that we

were restoring our strength *in order* to negotiate successfully with the other superpower that finally the time had
come to start.

So the next two months, July and August of 1983, wit-
nessed a kind of mini-thaw in U.S.-Soviet relations. It involved movement in three of the four areas of the new
agenda, with regional issues the exception. On June 18
Shultz informed Dobrynin of the President's decision to go
forward on the consulates and the exchanges agreement,
and Dobrynin conveyed Soviet acceptance on July 15. The
end of that month brought very quick conclusion of a new
long-term agreement on grains. The Soviets raised their
minimum purchase commitment by half, and while these
terms were not surprising, the speed with which they settled was. The last of the Pentecostals left the USSR in July.
In August the two governments negotiated a solution that
both could accept to the prickly case of a potential defector,
Andrei Berezhkov, who was also the son of a Soviet Embassy official. There was movement even in arms control.
Both sides made small shifts in their START positions, and
even in INF we were working hard on a number of new
positions when Andropov announced in late August that
the Soviets would destroy whatever missiles they agreed to
withdraw. None of these moves were world-shaking, but
taken together and compared to what had gone before, it
was a start.

Still, it was only a start. By mid-1983 the Reagan Administration had built the makings of a new American
political consensus on U.S.-Soviet relations into the
makings of a new policy approach, and it had discovered

that America had restored enough of its strength and confidence to begin implementing that approach. But that approach was not yet a policy program, and the
Administration did not yet have a partner for negotiations
on this new basis in Moscow.

Chapter 3

Introducing Gorbachev: U.S.-Soviet Relations 1983-1985

T his chapter follows the story of U.S.-Soviet relations
in the 1980s from the critical juncture of 1983 until
the end of 1985. These turned out to be the Reagan
Administration's middle years and Mikhail Gorbachev's
first, since he became General Secretary in March of 1985
and met with President Reagan in Geneva in November.
There had been a mini-thaw at the beginning of the period,
and there was fresh momentum at the end. But neither was
inevitable, and the path from one to the other was extremely crooked.

The first step taken was backward. The mini-thaw of
the summer of 1983 has now been forgotten, for relations
were promptly frozen over following the Soviet downing
of Korean Airlines (KAL) Flight 007 on August 31.

Looking back on the KAL crisis, we can see that it con-
firmed the Administration's new-found confidence in itself
and in America's capacity to deal with the Soviets. The

President arrived back in Washington from Santa Barbara to announce that he would not allow the Soviets to turn KAL into a bilateral U.S.-Soviet crisis, as they so clearly wished to do when they insisted that the airliner was a U.S. spy plane. He therefore rejected cabinet advice to freeze and cut relations across the board, in the good old way. It is certainly true that he led the chorus of world indignation about the killing of peaceful air travelers. But he also limited specific U.S. sanctions to steps that were clearly related to air travel, boycotting Aeroflot, canceling a cooperative agreement on transportation, and the like. Most significant of all, he sent his arms-control negotiators back to the negotiating tables in Geneva. There could not have been a sharper contrast with the across-the-board sanctions the Carter Administration had inflicted on the Soviets after Afghanistan and those Reagan himself imposed after Polish martial law.

At the time, however, KAL looked simply like another setback in relations. The "hot autumn" of 1983 was spent first on the KAL crisis and then on the struggle over INF deployment called for then by the 1979 NATO dual-track decision if negotiations were not yet successful. After U.S. deployments began, in November the Soviets walked out of both INF and START negotiations without agreeing to a resumption date. Andropov had last appeared in public on August 18, and he was seriously ill. On September 28 the Soviets issued an extraordinary statement in his name to the effect that "even if someone had any illusions about the possible evolution for the better of the U.S. administration, the latest developments have finally dispelled them."

After the walkout, in November and December the Soviet propaganda machine went into high gear with a war scare. It proclaimed to the Soviet people and the world that the United States was heading them toward nuclear war. And it was not all propaganda. It was later reported from inside that Soviet intelligence went on high alert at this time looking for U.S. war moves. Nor did it affect only the world; it also ate into Soviet opinion. A campaign of letters to President Reagan promoted by the Soviet authorities produced many spontaneous expressions of real fear from ordinary Soviets. Possibly, therefore, the war scare was getting out of hand. Whatever the reason, it stopped abruptly in mid-December, with a speech by Defense Minister Dimitriy Ustinov saying in effect that things were not so bad. But the whole autumn of 1983 added another heavy layer to the existing substrata of mistrust between the two countries.

The crust was hardened by the fact that the next year, 1984, was a U.S. presidential election year. President Reagan himself began it by holding out an olive branch to the Soviet Union. In a major address on January 16, he went through the three principles of the U.S. approach to the Soviet Union — strength, realism and negotiation — and the four parts of our new agenda for dialogue, but he put an altogether new stress on negotiation. Yet because it was an election year, it was hard for the Soviets and for many others as well to take that stress at face value. The timing alone made it sound too much like a mere election ploy. Soviet politics also made it hard for the Soviets to listen. Andropov was dying, and when he died in February and was succeeded by Brezhnev's old crony Konstantin Chernenko, Soviet energies were fixed for the nonce on the succession struggle. It took until mid-year to work out a kind of tandem holding arrangement between Chernenko and the younger, rising star of Gorbachev. For the time being, the Soviets stayed dug in on the policy status quo and stuck to their demand that the U.S. change its INF position before they would return to any nuclear arms-control negotiations at all.

In fact, the only arms-control negotiations the Soviets were willing to engage in were those in which the Europeans were also involved: MBFR talks in Vienna; the talks on chemical weapons talks in Geneva; and the talks on confidence-building measures in Europe going on in the CSCE context at Stockholm. From their point of view, the "battle for Europe" had not ended their defeat on INF deployments. But this refusal to negotiate bilaterally on nuclear arms was a political gift to the administration. The U.S. had only to say that it was ready to go back anytime to persuade the world that we and not the Soviets were the standard-bearers of nuclear arms control. Precisely because it was so firmly encamped on the high ground of public diplomacy, however, the Administration felt freer to be forthcoming on arms-control issues where it sat with its European allies. As an example, in April then-Vice President Bush presented a major proposal for a chemical weapons global ban in Geneva. Further, the Administration discovered a license to pile proposals for bilateral dialogue on the negotiating table. Most of them involved rather small, non-arms-control issues, cooperative agreements and the like, but there were even some hints of new directions in arms control: a framework proposal in START, an aborted mission to Moscow by former National Security Advisor Brent Scowcroft.

But month after month the Soviets stayed dug in, and in May they dug themselves in even further by boycotting our Los Angeles Olympics. It was a sudden decision, going against the grain of their thorough, visible preparations to come and win. In earlier days we would have reacted with shock and anger. Now our interpretation was that we were dealing with a hibernating bear. The London *Economist* reflected this interpretation when it put Chernenko on the cover under the heading "Goodbye, Cruel World!" and that in turn tickled the President. So he kept offering his olive branch. In the end he held it out four times that year, in his January 16 address, in the State of the Union later in the month, at Dublin in June, and again in June in a Washington conference on U.S.-Soviet exchanges. And meanwhile the list of concrete, constructive U.S. proposals got longer and longer.

For the last time in this story, it was Soviet stasis rather than activism that moved the U.S. forward, by confirming our confidence that we could handle the Soviet Union on a new and better basis if only we were strong and realistic. It was good politics — for U.S.-Soviet relations were not a controversial issue in the 1984 election campaign — but it also pointed the way toward a better diplomatic future. This time the general American approach generated in the Administration's first years took on the concrete form of specific proposals across the range of issues. The effect, in that summer of 1984, was to turn the Administration's impulses into an actual negotiating program. We had defined objectives that would be in our interest if they could be achieved, and these objectives were broadly accepted in American politics. Some were visionary, some were very down to earth, but together they constituted a detailed and comprehensive agenda for negotiation. And we were on the hook, if only the Soviets would respond.

Perhaps because they were reading the polls, perhaps because they were getting their ducks in a row at home, in June 1984 the Soviets began to respond. First, they started to pick up various bilateral proposals for dialogue on their merits. This had the effect of releasing the bilateral area of the agenda from political linkage, for it meant that the Soviets were permitting progress to take place *somewhere* even without progress on the arms-control "core issues." Because their overall line was to restore everything to its 1970s status, that was probably the easy part. Then, at the end of June, they suddenly proposed to begin negotiations in Vienna in September on what they called "space-strike weapons" — meaning the Strategic Defense Initiative (SDI), which was their main bugaboo at the time. The U.S. surprised everyone by responding overnight and by accepting the proposal, but only on condition that offensive weapons be discussed too. Such nimbleness would have been unthinkable a year before, and it drove the Soviets up against their own position that our INF position had to change for nuclear arms negotiations to resume. Counterproposals and counter-counterproposals went back and forth through July. What was impressive was not that these exchanges failed, but that they went on so long and that the positions of the two sides were converging at the end, even though they did not meet enough to permit agreement. And toward the end of the month Foreign Minister (and Politburo Member) Gromyko accepted our invitation to visit Washington during his trip to the fall UN General Assembly. It was understood that he would be meeting with the President.

During that September 1984 visit, Gromyko renewed the direct sounding of Ronald Reagan that had begun with the Pentecostalist issue in the spring of 1983 and then stopped with KAL. Gromyko did not come to do actual diplomatic business. Instead, he resolutely kept the talks at the philosophical level, boring in on what he called "the question of questions," the issue of peace and war, and each side's intentions on that issue. And he discovered that this was just the level the President liked best, where he was most at home and most eloquent. Ronald Reagan told Gromyko in those talks that he sincerely believed the Soviet Union threatened the United States; that while nuclear war could not be won and must never be fought, it was mistrust that produces weapons, rather than the other way around; and that to get at the weapons you have to get at the mistrust, and hence at the differences between the two societies, and hence at human rights. And Gromyko chose to take all this as substantial agreement between the leaders of the two countries at what the Soviets call the "level of principle."

In the practice of the highly centralized and hierarchical Soviet dictatorship, agreement at the "level of principle" is even more important than it is in our democracy. It sends a signal downward through the immense Soviet bureaucracy and is the enabling act that provides the policy cover for practical steps. We then proceeded to confirm the message Gromyko had heard, in two ways. First, even before the U.S. election, on October 18 in Los Angeles Secretary Shultz gave a major address on managing the U.S.-Soviet relationship. It reconfirmed the new policy framework that was emerging, including its four-part agenda and its altered, narrowed concept of linkage. Most of all, it stressed that we were in for the long haul, that our intention was to put relations with the Soviets on a stable and constructive basis for the long term. Then, on the day after his landslide reelection in November, Ronald Reagan sent out his olive branch once again, in a private letter to Chernenko. And this time the Soviets were ready with a swift and positive response. After some dickering, the two superpowers announced on November 22 — Thanksgiving Day — that the foreign ministers would meet in Geneva in January "to enter into new negotiations with the objective of reaching mutually acceptable agreements on the whole range of questions concerning nuclear and outer space arms." Describing the negotiations as "new" was something for the Soviets, to let them off their post-walkout hook on INF and START. The rest of the text was the U.S. counterproposal of late June. In its turn, the January meeting produced agreement to begin those new negotiations, on the agreed basis, in March. We were back in business even in arms control.

Also in March, General Secretary Konstantin Chernenko died and was succeeded at last by Mikhail Gorbachev. In a way, the Soviet succession period of the early 1980s had been fortunate for the Soviet elite, as it was for us. For them, it was a period when the general sense of crisis spreading in the late 1970s was consolidated and heightened without actual active new threats from us or from their neighbors. The succession process — the spectacle of ever older and weaker leaders following each other to a brief tenure and rapid death — humiliated them. Together with their own sense of isolation and decrepitude, the Reagan Administration's new rhetoric frightened them. But because our main priorities were in fact as domestic as theirs, the Soviets were frightened without actually being threatened. The period thus made everyone in the Soviet elite focus on the long-term dangers of continuing the status quo without requiring them really to react, and perhaps to overreact. In other words, it permitted them to generate the makings of a theory of why they were facing crisis and the makings of a program for addressing it in their own terms.

For our part, the succession gave us the luxury of restoring some strength and a great deal of self-confidence in a period when the Soviets were at a policy standstill, when they were not actively pushing out against our interests in new ways. It is true that we talked mainly to ourselves. But we used this dialogue among ourselves and with our allies, a dialogue driven by our own logic, to put together a solid conceptual framework and a comprehensive new agenda for dialogue. Of course, the results that would finally be needed to validate the new approach politically were not yet in. It was clear that the proof of the pudding would be in the eating. But by the time Gorbachev arrived in March 1985, there was a lot to work with.

And yet the road forward continued to be extremely crooked. The first step was auspicious. Vice President Bush and Secretary Shultz were impressed with Gorbachev when they met him at Chernenko's funeral that month. He spoke reflectively about the major changes in the world in recent years and about the need for both countries to think through the implications of those changes. We felt ready for that, as the whole purpose of the policy we had developed over four long years of Soviet passivity was to prepare us to deal with whatever their history turned up, and we felt it had been a successful policy. What we told ourselves at the time was that with the President's resounding reelection in November, Gorbachev's advent and the so-called new negotiations on nuclear and space systems, both the United States and the Soviet Union now had vigorous leaders who might be able to do real business. So the way ahead looked open. Yet there were still political problems with going down it.

The main new factor was obviously Soviet politics, as long as Soviet policy was standing pat. During the first Administration, what was happening domestically in the Soviet Union had not been much of a factor in our policy. Now, however, Soviet domestic affairs — Gorbachev's intentions, his prospects for surviving and prospering — were obviously going to be important again. But that in itself complicated our policymaking. Soviet politics under Gorbachev remain even more secretive and mysterious than our own. Gorbachev has not simply replaced one political culture with another. Rather, he has sought to change Soviet policies and politics by picking his way forward through the old terrain. That mix of old and new makes the story of superpower relations in the second Reagan term harder to tell. It also made U.S. policy harder to formulate.

Still, Gorbachev showed very early on that he was a real reformer. For one thing, he made it clear from the outset that he was genuinely experimental, that he was willing to try things and then, if they failed, to try something else. This went against the grain of the whole Soviet tradition in politics. Because the Soviet leadership's legitimacy depends on its claim to understand the laws of history rather than on an election mandate, it had to be right in everything it did. Gorbachev announced that he was willing to see if he was right by small steps. This was upsetting, because it meant that history could bless only the whole program, and only over time, rather than each of its parts, and right now.

On the other hand, Gorbachev's piecemeal experimentalism also had domestic political advantages. Like all members of the Soviet elite, he and the reformers around him were trained to command, and they overestimated the system's potential for quick change on command and underestimated the need for political management to achieve change. So it was just as well that they gave themselves some time and flexibility. More importantly, the new openendedness meant that every battle could be fought again, that no sectoral interest would ever be entirely down and out. In other words, it meant that the Gorbachev leadership would be willing to co-opt, to back off, to bargain. By promoting change, it activated political struggle, but by proceeding in experimental and piecemeal fashion, it also lowered the stakes of that struggle. And after sixty years of all-or-nothing politics in which a leader's political future depended on winning every battle, this was a political benefit for members of the elite that was as big in its way as Brezhnev's cadre stability.

Nevertheless, in 1985 that was for the future. Precisely because the stakes had always been so high, in Gorbachev's first year Soviet politics was still very much leadership struggle. Gorbachev came to power as a successor to Andropov, supported by the same, mainly national-security clienteles that had supported him: the police, the military, the foreign affairs establishment, sectors of the intelligentsia. His political problem was to extend that support out into the immense economic management apparatus that constitutes the bulk of the Soviet elite. And he had a deadline, the 27th Party Congress scheduled for early 1986. That Congress would elect a new Central Committee, and he wanted it to be "his" Central Committee, with a majority that owed him their places and would support his reform. No one was as yet talking about political reform. More and more of the elite agreed in principle that what the country needed was serious economic reform. The problem was that in practice economic reform frightened the very people whose support Gorbachev now hoped to gain.

Throughout 1985 the solution to this dilemma was to stay away from the details of economic reform and concentrate on personnel change. Into the Politburo Gorbachev co-opted a pool of high-level economic management talent, the West Siberian clientele of Andrei Kirilenko, a man who had been Brezhnev's heir-apparent until he retired honorably for genuine health reasons, and thereby left his clients politically available. But when it came to programs, Gorbachev concentrated on discipline, anti-corruption and anti-alcoholism. It was hoped that tightening up on economic performance in this way without changing the system would buoy productivity and put some new goods on the shelves. With the help of the first good harvest in several years, it probably did, on a one-shot basis. More importantly, attacking corruption and indiscipline was congenial to Gorbachev's national security clienteles, and it justified extensive personnel changes in the provinces. This was politically popular, for throwing the rascals out is always popular under new regimes. Because the tradition in the Soviet party was that many officeholders have an automatic right to Central Committee seats, the rascals' replacements were as likely as not to be at the Congress and to help Gorbachev. So there were all sorts of good reasons to keep the details of economic reform under wraps. But surely one main reason to do so was also to keep the fearful economic managers in line and sidestep struggles over resource allocations among major groups that would alienate support Gorbachev would need when the Congress met.

Foreign policy was part of the program, but in complicated ways. Here too Gorbachev wished to impart a sense of movement and change, but still without alienating support in the run-up to the Congress. He inherited a set of foreign policy positions and postures that were very hard to change, and the support of their authors. Moreover, Soviet leaders are expected to lead both at home and abroad. So even if Gorbachev's initial priorities were as domestic as the Reagan Administration's in 1981 — and they probably were — he did not have Reagan's luxury of simply working on the other superpower's external environment until he was ready to negotiate. He was handed a briefing book that had almost canonical force, but he had to engage.

Summitry promised a way out of the dilemma of how to move without changing positions. Given the leadership focus of Soviet politics at the time, summitry was a natural. The inclination to start at the top is one of the oldest and hardiest features of Soviet political culture. The system is hierarchical, and when Soviet leaders are faced with a construction problem their first impulse is to begin with the roof and leave the walls to subordinates who can be blamed for cave-ins. That helps account for the difficulty Soviet officials have with mixed relationships and with accidents, because for them every event and every position somehow reflects leadership intentions, and if these are not all good, they can only be all bad. It also helps explain their fondness for principles and for declarations of principles as a way around this difficulty. But it makes summits attractive. Now, in the spring of 1985, solid Soviet political reasons made summitry doubly attractive. The question of whether to meet at the highest level had almost disappeared from the U.S.-Soviet screen in the succession years, but the U.S. was definitely ready for it. Vice President Bush had, in fact, brought a summit proposal for Gorbachev to Chernenko's funeral. And even before Gorbachev became a key player in Soviet politics, Foreign Minister Gromyko had begun to sound out Ronald Reagan on his genuine intentions and had liked what he had heard. Summitry thus meant continuity as well as change. So Gorbachev immediately accepted, in principle.

Yet he temporized for over two months before nailing down the November dates to meet Reagan in Geneva, and we can see in retrospect that the problems were political rather than technical. U.S.-Soviet summitry was natural to both sides, both sides were ready in principle, but in practice there were difficulties.

To be sure, we did our share in creating them. Relations were far from genial. The specifics of arms control continued to limp forward. But in June, after years of mounting American political concern over Soviet violations of arms-control agreements, President Reagan put a year-end deadline on continued U.S. observance of the limits to our strategic arms deployments that were provided for in the unratified SALT II Treaty. This was a typical Washington compromise, what is called a Treaty of the Potomac, but to the Soviets it looked like one more American ultimatum, more "dictation."

However, many of the obstacles on the road to the summit were of Soviet origin. That spring they announced a unilateral moratorium on nuclear testing, but whatever its arms-control value the step was correctly seen as mainly a challenge. And the spring and summer were strewn with nasty and hostile incidents rooted in Soviet conduct: the killing of Major Arthur D. Nicholson, Jr. by Soviet soldiers in East Germany in March; the discovery of the Walker spy ring; the revelation that the Soviets had routinely used potentially dangerous "spy dust" to track our embassy personnel in Moscow; the curious defection and then redefection of the intelligence operative Vitaliy Yurchenko.

When issues like these surface in U.S.-Soviet relations, particularly in proximity to a high-level meeting, the air is immediately filled with dark suspicions that "certain circles" are trying to slow or prevent progress, to torpedo the event or its results. The centralized and secretive Soviets are particularly prone to such suspicion, but it is a two-way street: Americans have those suspicions too. In concrete cases it is very hard to run down the truth one way or the other. I have found that the best approach is to assume such incidents are natural in our relations, because accidents and malice as well are both natural where there is such a legacy of hostility and mistrust. I have also found that the best way to deal with them is on their merits. Working an issue on its merits often prevents it from becoming the firestorm that burns down everything in sight. By sending his arms-control negotiators back to the table even as he led world outrage over KAL 007, the President had set an example. By 1985 this approach was taking hold within the U.S. government.

Thus there were plenty of specific reasons in 1985 for why it was hard to get from principle to practice when it came to summitry. But it seems to me that the main obstacles on the Soviet side were of another kind and were lodged within the Soviet leadership. For summitry was all very well, and was even attractive in principle. But there was clearly a strong feeling in Moscow that a summit with the U.S. had to produce a substantive arms-control result involving a major U.S. concession on an issue of interest to the Soviet Union. A "fireside summit," a get-acquainted meeting between the two leaders without such an agreement, was a very comfortable concept for us. But at this early stage in Gorbachev's tenure, such a summit was still politically unacceptable to many Soviet leaders. And what they wanted as a precondition for summit "success" in 1985 was a U.S. concession on the President's SDI program.

Because we are not privy to the details, we must deduce the Soviet political problem from their actions. The key piece of evidence is that it was in late June, only the very day after Andrei Gromyko was elevated from his decades of stewardship over Soviet foreign policy to the titular state presidency, that the Soviets accepted our proposal to meet in Geneva November 19 and 20. And still they did not give up on SDI. On the contrary: Beginning then and continuing almost up to the summit itself, the whole apparatus — policy, propaganda, and leaks — insisted that only a concession from Reagan on SDI would make Geneva a "success."

Their argument was that they could not be expected to undertake tremendous reductions in strategic offensive weapons in START while we claimed the right to build strategic defenses as we saw fit, without guarantees that we would not use the program to put new offensive weapons in space, if only under another President. For President

Reagan this was not a problem. For him, reducing offensive nuclear weapons and building defenses against them were two sides of the same visionary coin. Together they would lift the threat of nuclear destruction hovering over mankind. But many in the West agreed with the Soviet argument on its merits. To make the point concretely, the Soviet negotiating position in Geneva linked START and INF reductions — one part of the President's "new thinking" — to limits on SDI — the other part — that would have had the effect of killing SDI politically, if not by treaty. In other words, the Soviets were insisting that President Reagan prove his good intentions and register agreement between the two leaderships at the "level of principle" by admitting a contradiction at the very heart of his dream.

As the Geneva Summit approached, it became clearer and clearer that Ronald Reagan would not do so. In October, we surprised the world by launching the so-called broad interpretation of the 1972 Treaty on Anti-Ballistic Missiles, or ABM, declaring our right to conduct testing and development of SDI as we wished. Although it was also decided that SDI research would go forward for the time being within the more restrictive "narrow interpretation," here was yet another unilateral assertion of U.S. rights on the very issue that the Soviets had identified as key to summit success. Shultz's preparatory meeting with Gorbachev in Moscow was stormy. It produced no movement. Instead, it appeared to augur trouble.

Then, a week before the leaders met, the Soviets retreated. Soviet spokesmen arriving in Geneva and those who stayed in Moscow suddenly proclaimed that the summit would be a success as a get-together of the two leaders, with only the small, practical agreements on non-arms-control issues that had already been prepared — the new exchanges agreement, perhaps something on civil aviation — to show for it.

And on that level Geneva was indeed a success. In the first meeting of superpower leaders in more than six years, the fearsome Ronald Reagan reiterated that nuclear war cannot be won and must never be fought; that any war between the two countries, nuclear or conventional, must be prevented; that neither side should seek military superiority; and that they should start with 50 per cent reductions in strategic nuclear arms, the goal set forth in his Eureka speech over two years before. Even more important from the Soviet point of view — because such declarations have political value in the Soviet tradition — Reagan and Gorbachev signed a joint statement that put these views solemnly on the international record.

Moreover, although Reagan would not be moved on SDI he told Gorbachev that it was not his purpose to threaten the Soviet Union. On the contrary, he said, he was worried about the Soviet threat, and he was dedicated to reducing the mistrust that made both countries afraid and kept them armed. Reagan was learning as we went that the Soviet Union was a real place and that Gorbachev was like himself insofar as he was a real politician. Even though Gorbachev led a dictatorship, he was a leader who faced resistance and opposition, as well as a man who could both talk and listen. And the President took Gorbachev at his word when he said he had a real problem with SDI, that it was genuinely hard for the Soviets to reduce existing offensive weapons without guarantees that defense would not mask development of new offensive weapons. At both the level of principle and the level of understanding between the leaders, therefore, there was progress, and important progress. It seemed to Gorbachev a conversation worth pursuing. And he therefore accepted the U.S. proposal for home-and-home summits in Washington and Moscow. The timing was not specified, but 1986 and 1987 were understood. So Geneva was only a "fireside summit," but it was a good start.

And yet the Geneva Summit saddled Gorbachev with a dilemma that determined the shape of U.S.-Soviet relations through the rest of the Reagan administration. He not only dropped in advance the precondition for a successful summit he had himself proclaimed, on SDI; he then returned to Moscow committed to two more summits with Reagan without any guarantee that they would produce a substantial arms-control result either. And now he had to achieve such a result without setting new preconditions that could backfire again as the SDI precondition had. After the long years of tension, Geneva was popular with the Soviet people. But U.S.-Soviet equality was reestablished in form rather than in substance as the Soviet leadership had defined substance for over a decade. Whether Geneva was a political success in the elite, where it counted for the Congress and the new Central Committee, was therefore much more problematic. In the next chapter I will describe how this dilemma was addressed and where it led. It led first, albeit over a characteristically crooked path, to the Reagan-Gorbachev meeting at Reykjavik, and in odd, specific ways, Reykjavik has led toward a new and better U.S.-Soviet relationship as the 1980s end.

Chapter 4

To Reykjavik and Beyond:
U.S.-Soviet Relations
1986-1988

I n the aftermath of the Geneva Summit, Soviet policy toward the United States was driven by the dilemma of how to get an American assurance that the next summit would produce a substantial arms control result without actually making such an assurance a precondition to nailing down final agreement to meet.

In a movement that would become characteristic both at home and abroad, Gorbachev's next step went sideways. On January 15 of 1986, he unveiled a visionary program for eliminating all nuclear weapons by the year 2000. It had some elements of interest to us. It built on the Geneva joint statement that nuclear war cannot be won and must never be fought, and it also dropped the long-standing Soviet demand for including British and French weapons in INF results. But it was very much the kind of program Soviet leaders produce to prove they are leaders, a kind of election plank after the election rather than before. In fact, it was to be the first of a series of such Gorbachev programs over the next several years: for reducing conventional arms in Europe, in April; for Asia, at Vladivostok in July; later on, for northern Europe at Murmansk, for southern Europe at Belgrade. By their nature such programs are all mishmashes of old and new Soviet proposals. They are therefore very easy to dismiss as propaganda, and anything concrete in them takes time to negotiate. In the case of the nuclear program, the time remaining before the Soviet Party Congress was too short for that.

And when the 27th Party Congress finally met the next month, it turned out that all Gorbachev's efforts of 1985 had not been good enough to get him a solid majority in the new Central Committee that was elected. His majority in the Politburo was solid enough for the policies he had defined up to that point, but in the Central Committee it was solid enough only to defend him from ouster of the kind that Khrushchev engineered against the "anti-party group" in 1957, or that Khrushchev himself then suffered in 1964. The new Central Committee could be counted on to keep Gorbachev in office but not to support any specific program for reform.

Gorbachev was thus condemned to build coalitions issue by issue, and after the Congress he began to move in a number of new directions. In 1985 economic reform had been a slogan rather than a program. Now its details began to be fleshed out, but still without tackling resource allocation among sectors and thereby identifying the major groups in Soviet politics whose budget oxen would have to be gored. "New political thinking" was proclaimed, and under that rubric *glasnost*, the opening up of broad new opportunities to debate, criticize, and publicize problems. New thinking seemed a suspiciously empty slogan to outsiders who did not understand the critical need in Soviet politics to begin with an agreed ideological line. It was true that the content remained to be filled in, but it was a license for all kinds of ideological shifts that are absolutely necessary preconditions for changes in actual Soviet policies. As for *glasnost*, in practical terms it appeared to bring in new support only from the intelligentsia, the most dependent and easily controllable sector of the Soviet body politic. But in fact it also served to discredit conservatism in general and conservatives in particular in the personnel struggle. And its popularity permitted the Gorbachev leadership to launch the politically loaded theory that the political players consisted of themselves and the people, pitted against the intervening lump of the apparatus.

In the longer term these new departures would help Gorbachev and reform, but in the short term they did not resolve the post-Geneva dilemma over how to deal with the United States. For our part we were cheerfully calling on the Soviets to fix the dates for the Washington Summit in 1986 that they had agreed to in Geneva. The substance of the relationship continued to be very mixed, but we at least were willing to talk about everything, anytime, anywhere. We were just not willing to lock in an outcome before the meeting itself. By contrast, the Soviets looked fussy and insincere, because after Geneva it was doubly important to them to make sure beforehand that the next summit would produce a substantial arms-control result, but they could not actually ask straight out for what they wanted for fear of creating another precondition like the one on SDI that had blown up on them. And there was no mechanism in place for building to another summit and working out the Soviet problem along the way.

This was because the Soviets were still very resistant to the four-part agenda, to the concept of discussing all the issues between the two countries — the good, the bad, and the ugly — on a regular basis. There were no doubt many reasons for this resistance. The American paternity of the concept was probably one of them. Beyond that, however, many Soviets certainly felt that if they discussed human rights with us they would be acquiescing in illegitimate outside interference in their domestic affairs. They had also had bitter experience with what they saw as empty dialogue, fruitless discussion that the Americans then pointed to in order to prove to a skeptical domestic public that all was well because talks were going on. They were especially wary that we would use exchanges on *non*-arms-control issues to downgrade or bury arms control, which was still "the question of questions" as far as they were concerned.

Whatever the reason, in the spring of 1986 Soviet resistance to comprehensive, regular dialogue made it impossible for them to work off the horns of their post-Geneva dilemma. Consequently, the relationship wandered. After Geneva no meeting of foreign ministers was foreseen before the next UN General Assembly session in September. When one was finally scheduled for April, the Soviets felt obliged to cancel it beforehand to express displeasure over the Libyan bombing. There was no pattern. In March we had told the Soviets they would have to draw down their intelligence-heavy UN Mission by over a hundred staff members in thirteen months, with the first departures due in October. May was the month of the Chernobyl disaster. We offered sympathy and assistance, but late in the month we also announced that Soviet violations of arms-control treaties freed us from the SALT II restraints on strategic weapons deployments that we had previously observed. Partly in response, the Soviets turned up the volume of the propaganda campaign challenging us to join their nuclear test moratorium. Over the summer the rolling thunder on testing reached such a pitch that the Soviets seemed to be turning the moratorium into another summit precondition, and thus to be unlearning the painful pre-Geneva lesson that preconditions do not work. The situation was all very murky and frustrating. And no practical way out of it was visible on the horizon.

But there was a way out, and the movement came from both sides.

The Soviets moved first, and they moved on both substance and form. In May and June their arms control delegation in Geneva announced adjustments in Soviet positions that seemed for the first time to take into account major American concerns. However, this in itself would not have been enough to break through the murk. The Geneva negotiations were conducted in a public diplomacy fishbowl and under tight instructions from capitals. They therefore proceeded very slowly. They simply could not produce the assurance of a substantial arms-control result that Gorbachev needed to go to the summit in 1986. Something more was required.

So the key Soviet move had to do with form. Their specialty was top-down policymaking; they were less good at building the walls under the roof. Now, in a June letter to President Reagan, Gorbachev proposed moving the dialogue forward on all issues "in [what he called] all normal channels," and suggested that the foreign ministers should review progress across the board when they met in September. When Deputy Foreign Minister Aleksandr Bessmertnykh arrived in Washington in July, he followed up on Gorbachev's proposal by proposing home-and-home experts' meetings in Moscow and Washington on all four agenda areas for the month of August. Because the Soviets are European enough to hold August sacred for vacation, we knew they were serious. Their idea, Bessmertnykh said, was that the experts should focus on what we have in common rather than on what divides us; in September the ministers should then review the experts' work to see if a basis existed for subsequent decisions by the leaders as to whether to go to the summit. What all this meant was that the Soviets were playing back to us *our* formula of comprehensive experts' dialogue as a way of addressing their post-Geneva summitry dilemma. They were proposing to deal with that dilemma in three bites — first experts, then ministers, then leaders — rather than whole hog. And because it was the American formula, we accepted immediately.

So the Soviets were moving down the level of dialogue and broadening it out to include our whole agenda.

Meanwhile, and independently, we moved up, and on their favored terrain of arms control. President Reagan now intervened directly in the substance of what they considered "the core issue," strategic and space arms. We had proved our talent for laying brick; what had been missing — and in a presidential system — was hands-on presidential involvement. Now, in a July 25 letter to Gorbachev, the President imposed on his squabbling subordinates a position for the START and space talks that he had developed himself.

It turned out that Reagan had listened in Geneva when Gorbachev had explained the problem he had with deep offensive reductions as long as there were no firm limits on SDI. And while the President remained firmly attached to SDI, he wanted to help Gorbachev out. He had offered to share SDI technology, and that offer was still open, but Gorbachev had made clear that he was not persuaded it was serious. So Reagan was willing to try something else. He himself was not attached to the ABM Treaty of 1972. It set limits to his cherished SDI program, and because the numbers of strategic offensive weapons had ballooned rather than shrunk in the years since it was signed, it looked to him like a license to build them rather than an incentive to reduce them. But in order to make the U.S. deal with his problem, Gorbachev was linking offensive reductions to strict observance of the ABM Treaty over a set period. So with everyone's clearance, including that of the Joint Chiefs of Staff, Reagan told Gorbachev he would be willing to observe the ABM Treaty over such a period if

Gorbachev would agree under certain conditions to eliminate not just some but *all* ballistic missiles.

Thus, by late July 1986, for the first time in the decade both the United States and the Soviet Union now had active roofmakers and active bricklayers. And even though they were without a blueprint, they also had a mechanism and a work program for dealing with all the issues on the four-part agenda. This meant they had found a formula for conducting relations as a process. In the months that followed they succeeded in turning that formula into a pattern of practice, and that practice was one key to the achievements of subsequent years. But it was hard to do, and circumstance was once again the midwife.

August 1986 was no vacation. The experts spent the month in talks on their specialties in Washington and Moscow, and these talks went very well. The fact that the ministers would review their work spurred them on, and once all issues are on the table no single issue is critical, so all are easier to handle. Even in arms control there was concrete and surprising progress.

But at the end of the month the prototypical firestorm in U.S.-Soviet relations blew up. We arrested a Soviet agent, Gennadiy Zakharov, in New York, and in retaliation the Soviets detained an American journalist, Nicholas Daniloff, in Moscow. This country erupted in massive and vociferous indignation. And the October deadline was approaching for the drawdown of the first of the hundred or so Soviet UN Mission personnel due out by April 1988.

So when Shultz and Shevardnadze met in mid-September, they had to deal not only with the results of the experts' review — to see if there was a basis for their leaders' going to the summit — but also with this Daniloff/Zakharov/UN personnel crisis — to see if there was a basis for any kind of positive relationship at all. Earlier such a crisis would have overwhelmed the process. This time the ministers succeeded in keeping diplomacy and crisis management running on separate tracks, together but in parallel. We saw in retrospect that the KAL crisis of 1983 was the successful test of restored U.S. self-confidence, confidence in our American capacity to keep pursuing objectives we had defined for ourselves in relations with the Soviets while dealing with crisis in one area. That was a major achievement, but it was unilateral, all on the U.S. side. Now the Daniloff/Zakharov crisis of 1986 tested the capacity of *both* countries to deal with good and bad issues at the same time. And they passed the test with flying colors.

But it was a close thing, and out of that close thing popped the meeting between Reagan and Gorbachev at Reykjavik. In the midst of the Daniloff/Zakharov negotiations, Gorbachev proposed to Reagan that they meet in either Britain or Iceland, and thus in neither Washington nor Moscow, as they had agreed in Geneva. Once the crisis was resolved, Reagan accepted Reykjavik. The Daniloff/Zakharov flare-up certainly reminded the Soviets that they had not yet found a reliable way to guarantee the substantial arms-control result they needed for a Washington summit.

On September 13, just before Shevardnadze arrived in the U.S., Soviet Foreign Ministry spokesman Gennadiy

Gerasimov suggested that since the Americans were so dug in on nuclear testing, perhaps an INF treaty could be signed separately at the summit, and that this would satisfy the Soviet requirement for "one or two" substantial agreements there. But Gerasimov was ahead of Soviet policy, and time was running out. In that perspective Gorbachev's proposal to meet in a third country was a flight forward out of his dilemma, a make-or-break effort to square the circle he had built for himself nearly a year before.

Gorbachev's negotiating brief at Reykjavik certainly had a go-for-broke quality about it. Over two momentous days, he set out for Reagan an offer of reductions in offensive nuclear weapons that went beyond anything contemplated before, but it was absolutely conditional on an SDI concession. As in the run-up to Geneva, Gorbachev sought once again to drive the two parts of Reagan's dream of a non-nuclear world — elimination of offensive weapons and secure defenses against them — up against each other. This time, however, he pressured his case with concrete and specific quids rather than the general political threat of "failure." And on the basis of what Gorbachev did at Reykjavik and afterward, we can speculate that his instructions also said that if he did not succeed, then all the offers on offensive weapons were to come off the table, were to become as if they had never been.

Of course Gorbachev did not succeed at Reykjavik, any more than he succeeded before Geneva. In the end the President was unwilling to accept any contradiction between the two parts of his dream and to face the conservative backlash that was sure to greet him at home if he did. The trouble was that while Gorbachev had all-or-nothing instructions, and while he certainly did not get all, he also got a great deal more than nothing. Ronald Reagan struggled mightily to put his two-part dream in a form Gorbachev could tolerate and share. And he gave Gorbachev concrete proof of his willingness actually to reduce American nuclear arms. Since Geneva the Soviets had taken Reagan at his word, had assumed he was sincere. This showed, for instance, when they insisted that they wished to limit but not kill SDI, because they knew he was attached to it. But Reagan had never given them proof positive that he was really willing to do what was necessary to eliminate U.S. as well as Soviet offensive systems. And at Reykjavik he did.

The proof did not come over START, and certainly not over SDI. On START, the President returned to the proposal in his July 25 letter to eliminate all ballistic missiles over an agreed period of strict observance of the ABM Treaty, which he now extended to ten years. The two leaders then argued at length over what to do with offensive weapons during the second five years of this period, after the initial 50 per cent reductions they had agreed to at Geneva. Out of frustration over their inability to agree, they then fled up to the level of principle — the principle of eliminating all nuclear weapons — and finally returned to earth over SDI, on which the meeting broke down that Sunday evening.

So the proof of Reagan's goodwill was not in the areas of strategic arms or space. Rather it came earlier in the day, on INF. The Soviets had been blowing hot and cold about linking the conclusion of an INF agreement to agreements on START and space. In their Reykjavik package they returned to that linkage with a vengeance. But it was also true that the INF negotiations were the most advanced, with the most specific issues to be resolved. These had to do with Soviet acceptance of an equal global ceiling covering their SS-20's in Asia and a U.S. right to deploy in the United States, but very much outside Europe. If agreement could be reached, Europe at least would to be free of INF. All through Saturday and into Sunday morning Gorbachev pressed the President repeatedly to say whether he was *really* willing to forgo U.S. INF in Europe, whether the allies or the Congress would not insist on having some. And on Sunday morning, after the President had repeatedly said he was willing to eliminate them entirely, Gorbachev accepted the deal. It was not the deal he had been sent to get, but it was real, and important.

So on Sunday night after the breakdown, both we and the Soviets had real political problems. Our problem was how to prevent SDI from looking to world opinion like the single obstacle to fantastic nuclear arms reductions. The Soviets could be counted on to insist that it was, both because they believed it and because it was to their advantage to convince others that it was true. But Gorbachev's problem was even tougher. If he indeed came to Reykjavik with all-or-nothing instructions, as I have speculated, and had gotten something important, rather than either all or nothing, then he had to choose between taking all his offers off the table and leaving them on. If he left them on he would be breaking his instructions. But if he took them off he would be risking a repetition of the 1983-1985 situation, after the Soviet walkout from Geneva, when for over a year we had pounded the Soviets with the claim that we and not they were the flag-bearers of arms control. And in Gorbachev's and Shultz's separate press conferences that Sunday night, they found the same solution to their separate problems. Both proclaimed that their Reykjavik offers remained on the table and that negotiations based on those offers would go on.

But that solution was comfortable for us and very uncomfortable for the Soviet leadership. To prove that SDI was not the only roadblock, all we had to do was show that there had been much progress at Reykjavik, but also a lot of honest disagreement left over. To prove that SDI *was* the only roadblock, the Soviets had to re-create the all-or-nothing situation that Reykjavik had not produced. That meant claiming that everything had been agreed except SDI and insisting that nothing else could be done until the Americans changed on SDI. When Soviet emissaries fanned out to brief the West Europeans, they were shocked to find that what bothered Western Europe was not SDI but the Soviet insistence on making INF progress conditional on START and space results. It took them the better part of a week to develop the position that INF negotiations could proceed but could not conclude until all three agreements were ready to be signed together. And they spent the next months, through the Shultz-Shevardnadze meeting in Vienna in early November and beyond, trying to recoup.

91

This time the deadlock was broken by American politics. The day before Shultz and Shevardnadze met in Vienna, the Republicans surrendered the U.S. Senate to the Democrats once again, and a Beirut paper revealed that the United States had been secretly supplying arms to Iran to help get our hostages out of Lebanon. The Iran-Contra scandal that then erupted forced the Soviets to decide whether or not they wanted to do business with Ronald Reagan after all. At the level of principle the answer came quickly. Coming out of the Vienna standoff, on November 10 Shevardnadze told the press that despite U.S. backtracking, Geneva and Reykjavik had proved one can do business with President Reagan, who would be staying in power for two more years. The weakening of the Reagan presidency in Iran-Contra may even have helped by cutting Reagan down to size. But in practice it also invited temporizing. For the time being the standoff continued. It was only in January 1987 that we began to get hints that the Soviets were preparing to delink INF from the Reykjavik package again. But Gorbachev then passed up the natural occasion to do the deed, an East-West peace forum in Moscow in mid-February. So it was only on February 28, the day after Howard Baker was named White House Chief of Staff, that they announced INF could go forward to conclusion on its own. Partly, as usual, this was for the Europeans. But it also meant the Soviets had finally satisfied themselves that Ronald Reagan, though weakened, was once again operational.

Reykjavik had proved that Reagan was really willing to negotiate on nuclear arms, even though the proof was only in INF. Like Geneva, it was popular with the Soviet public. And it showed Gorbachev as a leader dealing with the American President as an equal and getting some results, which was also important to the elite. But the Soviet elite had much more on its plate in 1987 than just superpower relations.

By 1987 it was becoming clear that Gorbachev's economic reform at home, with its focus on the huge, complicated industrial management system, was running into the sand. So Gorbachev once more shifted gears. First, the time projection for economic reform was stretched out to around the year 2000. This matched the January 1986 program's target date for eliminating nuclear weapons, and it gave the leadership more time. Second, within the economic program there was new attention to two areas where reform might be easier than in industry and might bring a quicker welfare payoff. These were services, via encouragement of the cooperative sector, and agriculture. Third, the leadership's argument that it was engaged in a pincer movement with the people against the bureaucrats was fleshed out by the concept of political "democratization." Stymied on economic reform because of inadequate gains on the personnel front during and after the 1986 Party Congress, Gorbachev began to use the new welfare orientation in economics and "democratization" in politics to rally mass support for reform, in order to lay the groundwork for getting the kind of people he needed in order to move on.

But the price of this turn to politics was political tension, and in 1987 such tension surfaced in a major way and escalated even into the Politburo. Gorbachev used the landing of Matthias Rust's Cessna in Red Square to get himself a new military leadership, but it was not enough. It was in 1987 that Yegor Ligachev emerged as a kind of shadow standard-bearer for those who feared the political reform that Gorbachev now believed was needed if there was to be successful economic restructuring.

By 1987, therefore, there was finally a level playing field between the superpowers, but Reagan was weakened and into the homestretch of his presidency, and for Gorbachev tension on the home front was rising into the higher reaches of Soviet political life. The result, on both sides, was a lowering and shifting of expectations in their relations.

In the United States a new policy team was in place. Shultz was joined by Howard Baker as Chief of Staff, Colin Powell as National Security Advisor, and Frank Carlucci as Secretary of Defense. Slowly the passion drained out of policymaking on the Soviet Union and lodged instead in the Congress and the rest of the political system, which were now moving toward the 1988 election year. In the Soviet Union domestic politics also loomed larger, but "new political thinking" had now taken on a life of its own. It spread to foreign policy, and in foreign policy it now went far beyond arms control. The Soviet reform impulse was starting to produce results on the human rights issues the U.S. had identified as important: emigration, treatment of political and religious dissent, examination of Soviet laws and regulations to bring them in line with the country's international commitments. In foreign policy, even if arms control moved slowly, "new thinking" and developments on the ground combined to produce new and more constructive Soviet inputs into certain Third World crisis situations, the regional issues of the U.S.-Soviet agenda. With the principles in place and more to offer in practice, the Soviets grew more comfortable with the four-part agenda and positively attached to regular dialogue on all issues.

The foreign ministers now met frequently, and they were accompanied and indeed preceded by swarms of experts in all agenda areas. These meetings became the boiler room of the relationship. They provided deadlines for decision making in the two bureaucracies; vehicles for taking decisions that were ripe; fora for floating suggestions and ideas; places to exchange views for the record, to foreshadow changes of position, to identify specific interests, to take credit for moves you were making anyway. Agreements were now signed at these meetings as well as at the summit, for instance on nuclear risk reduction centers and on cooperation in peaceful outer space activities, in basic sciences, in combatting international narcotics trafficking. Other agreements, say on joint experiments in nuclear testing, or on prior notification of intercontinental ballistic missile (ICBM) and submarine-launched ballistic missile (SLBM) launches, originated there. The last tough INF issues — West German Pershing IA's, and verification — were tinkered out by the foreign ministers and their aides as much as by the negotiators in Geneva. Discussion of human rights cases and issues was a regular feature. It was after such meetings that we saw

Soviet movement on political and religious prisoners, on radio jamming, on AIDS disinformation. And they regularly produced the bilateral work programs that served each bureaucracy as a checklist for further work on the specifics between meetings. It was in the steady grinding of this intermediate-range machinery that U.S.-Soviet relations ceased to lurch from summit to summit and became a process.

Like us, therefore, but a half decade after us, the Soviets finally came to see that results were mainly important as validations of a process of dialogue and interaction which had larger political purposes and larger political effects, but which in turn helped produce the concrete results. By circuitous paths, both sides converged on a combination of leadership dialogue, working-level process and the four-part agenda as a new basis for their relations. It was on that basis that the INF Treaty was negotiated through 1987, signed at the Washington Summit in December and shepherded through the U.S. political thicket to Senate ratification in April 1988, in time for Reagan and Gorbachev to exchange the instruments of ratification in Moscow in May.

To be sure, there were still hiccups which showed that beneath the smoother surface Soviet politics was still a factor at work when it came to relations with the United States.

In October 1987, with all the last main INF issues resolved and the treaty practically ready for signature, Gorbachev suddenly announced to Shultz in Moscow that the INF Treaty would not be enough to justify coming to

Washington. In other (albeit unspoken) words, SDI was back again. This happened the day after the storm in the Soviet Central Committee over party maverick Boris Yel'tsin, and we had to assume that Gorbachev's college try was somehow related to it. Shultz was impassive, and the Western press reaction ran from bemusement to indignation. No one understood what the Soviets were up to, but it was up to them to come off it. Within a week Shevardnadze was in Washington to say the INF-only summit was back on track, and Gorbachev's December visit fell quickly into place.

Gorbachev's last college try under the Reagan Administration came seven months later, during the Moscow Summit. This time it focused on conservative principles in general rather than just SDI in particular. In their first one-on-one meeting in Moscow, without any advance warning, Gorbachev sprang a traditional Soviet-style general statement on Reagan. It included all the old chestnuts of Soviet diplomacy of the 1970s and some new ones: no military solutions to political problems; peaceful coexistence; non-interference in internal affairs; and free choice of socio-political systems. It could have been written by Gromyko in what was now called "the period of stagnation." Predictably, we turned it down, and Gorbachev vented his displeasure in public as well as in private. But as he had the previous October, he refused to let the turndown stand in the path of the new process, and the summit went on to a successful conclusion.

So in the end the Soviets still needed an arms-control result if they were to join us in putting relations on a new and better basis; but finally INF suffered, and INF in turn became largely symbolic of the larger new realities it had helped create. In 1988 the main international action involving the two countries was, in fact, outside bilateral relations in their strict sense. In February Gorbachev announced that Soviet troops would be fully withdrawn from Afghanistan within a year. The Soviets began to work actively for the political settlement being negotiated under U.S. auspices in southern Africa. It was not unnatural to see the action shift elsewhere, for in a U.S. election year triumphs in direct superpower relations on the order of the INF Treaty were just not in the cards. Superpower politics could provide no real relief from domestic politics. Gorbachev's college tries with Shultz and Reagan suggest that they may in fact have increased some tensions at home even if they softened others. As in America, therefore, 1988 was a preeminently domestic political year for Gorbachev, but in the Soviet context that made it the first great year of political reform and high-level personnel shifts.

Gorbachev kept control of the Soviet domestic agenda, as he had before and and has since (as of early 1990). A special Party Conference was scheduled for June 1988, and in the first half of the year he kept the political system wrapped around the axle the conference's mandate, and especially its mandate to make personnel changes. By early May it was already clear that the conference would not change personnel. But when it met Gorbachev still achieved an impressive political half-loaf. First, he turned traditionally hierarchical and secretive Soviet politics on their side by having Yel'tsin and "Second Secretary"

Ligachev debate each other in public and as equals, with Gorbachev himself in the middle, which is where the smart politician wants to be. Second, on the last day, without any prior debate, he sprang a whole new political reform program on the assembled delegates. It provided for real elections, for a new working legislature, and for a new presidency whose incumbent would be very hard to change by palace coup. The delegates then passed this program by a unanimous show of cards.

In other words, Gorbachev used the old politics to introduce a new system that would allow him to circumvent the old-fashioned obstruction his program was facing. Then, at the end of September, Gorbachev sprang an old-fashioned personnel palace coup himself. He established commissions to replace the powerful Central Committee Secretariat departments, but without defining their functions. He exiled his most conservative-sounding Politburo colleagues, Ligachev and KGB chief Viktor Chebrikov, to these commissions. And he brought new people beholden to him into both the new bodies and the Politburo itself.

In foreign policy, without the prospect of thrilling new forward steps in relations with the United States, the Gorbachev leadership spent 1988 basically preparing for the future, as we now see in retrospect. It continued to work with Ronald Reagan, but its objective was not so much to squeeze the last concrete results out of the process before he stepped down as to commit his successor to that process. And the Soviets began to flesh out the military and foreign policy "new thinking" generated over the previous two years, in the form of new policy proposals.

Gorbachev's visit to New York on December 7 did both things. Addressing the UN in the morning, Gorbachev announced substantial Soviet unilateral cuts in conventional forces in Europe, Asia, and the USSR. Then he went to lunch with both the President and the Vice President (and President-elect) on Governor's Island in New York harbor.

The meeting on Governor's Island has been called the "ultimate power lunch." It looked back on eight years in which the two superpowers, first separately, then together, had put in place a new and broader approach to dealing with each other and the mechanisms for achieving results that would support that approach politically at home. Whatever their ultimate intentions, whatever the differences in history, ideology, and interest that divided and would continue to divide them, however different the paths they had traveled and the directions they wished to go, the United States and the Soviet Union had arrived at this modest but good result. And that result, their leaders hoped, boded well for the future — their own future, to be sure, but also the future of their countries and the world.

Gorbachev's UN General Assembly announcement of unilateral Soviet troop cuts also looked both backward and forward. On the one hand, it was only the latest step in East-West debate and negotiation over the conventional force balance that had gone on for nearly two decades. In their specifics, conventional arms issues still masked the fundamentals of the East-West division of Europe, where the Cold War began. On the other hand, the way these issues were handled was also getting closer to those fundamentals. So Gorbachev's New York visit also said in symbolic form that the two superpowers had made enough progress on the traditional issues to begin to step up to the causes of the East-West confrontation the world had lived with for going on two generations. We had spent the 1980s putting the 1970s behind us. We had done so creatively and productively. But we were now ready to move on to really tough problems, like the division of Europe. I would like in my next two chapters to tell the complex story of how the division of Europe evolved as an international issue in the postwar world, and how it ripened in the 1980s to the point where we could afford to be so ambitious.

Chapter 5

Economism and Its Agony:
The Division of Europe
at the Turn of the 1980s

During the 1980s the division of Europe was not so much a test case in U.S.-Soviet relations as a problem for the international system with a hidden, heavy, and difficult life of its own. It was harder to deal with politically and is harder to describe and understand analytically than even the superpower relationship. Everyone knows and cares a lot about the superpowers. The problems, the crises, the solutions in their relations are daily front-page news. The division of Europe is different. Here the problems are usually muffled because everyone involved has reasons to avert their gaze from them. We think of them mainly in terms of crises, sudden eruptions that must be dealt with but that then subside, leaving things as they were. American thinking in particular is crisis-prone and crisis-bound. We recall what we know about the division of Europe when we recall where we were when some terrible East European explosion occurred. I was a student in Paris in November 1956, when angry crowds stormed French Communist Party headquarters after the Soviet reconquest of Budapest. A week after arriving in Warsaw in August 1968, my family and I were awakened by Polish planes taking off to join the invasion of Czechoslovakia. In December 1981 I was called back from Christmas vacation to join the State Department task force set up to deal with Polish issues after martial law was declared. All these explosions used to seem hopeless; now we would like to believe that they are hopeless no longer, but we cannot be sure. What remains true is that explosion is all we remember, and therefore all we know. Our consciousness of the East-West division in Europe is vivid, but it is also intermittent, and therefore fleeting.

Now the shape of Europe's division is changing in momentous ways. But to understand that change, it must be described and understood in its own terms, in terms of *change* and not just crisis. That means thinking about the division of Europe anew and filling in the gaps in our thinking between the crises. That is what I shall attempt to do in this and the next chapter. In this one I shall try to analyze Europe's division as a problem for the international system as it developed in the decades since World War II and as it stood in the late 1970s. Such analysis is the necessary prelude to the story in the next chapter of how the system dealt with the problem in the 1980s and perhaps brought itself to the threshold of new resolutions.

Ten years ago, at the turn of the 1980s, it was massively difficult even to define the problem in terms that would permit the international system to deal with it in new ways.

In the first place, political systems like things simple, and the division of Europe was complex. It also involved many parties for whom the stakes were at least as high as for the superpowers. The United States and the Soviet Union saw things globally, and if they so chose they could afford to define the division of Europe as one of many "regional issues" in their relations. However, they were not then defining it as such an issue, and this was partly because it shared in spades a feature of those so-called regional issues that they *were* talking about. By their nature, regional issues are issues where the superpowers have interests and influence but where they cannot by themselves determine the course of developments; regional parties themselves must do most of the work. But in Europe the other players were the superpowers' most important and closest allies. The superpowers had learned over a bloody half century that they need friends and allies and must listen to them, and nowhere more so than in that part of the world where two world wars and the Cold War had begun. But if you are a superpower, listening comes hard.

Moreover, as the division of Europe then stood, most of the interests involved supported continuation of a status quo that had emerged in the first postwar decade and had been adjusted enough in the mid-1950s to give it another whole generation of unhappy but useful life.

At its base, the division reflected structural differences between the two parts of Europe, just as it perpetuated them. When the Soviet and American armies met at the Elbe River in 1945, to the west of them lay countries that were indeed bled and ruined but that had been the most

for important message
turn to page 153

advanced, the most urbanized, the most industrialized, the most educated, and the most powerful nations in the world. To the east lay countries whose elites had only dreamed of matching those to the West. Compared to Western Europe, Eastern Europe was underurbanized and under-industrialized. It was poor in the resources that have constituted the sinews of economic strength and political power in the modern world. Its predominantly peasant societies had been governed mainly through self-selected and self-perpetuating bureaucracies. Although some elites had strong national traditions, national communities had in fact been weak and had encompassed the bulk of the population only in quite recent times. Politics had been an activity for the few, while the many had sought mainly to be left alone to sustain and secure their families, as the only reliable framework for human activity.

Eastern Europe was in fact the world's first under-developed area. This was the Europe that the Red Army conquered in 1944 and 1945 and that the Soviet Union was determined to use to escape its ruinous international isolation. Eastern Europe was to be the finest fruit of the Red Army's great victory over Hitler: The Soviets intended to make it the guarantee that such a war would never again have to be fought. It was to provide the USSR with a "socialist camp" to lead. This would prove that Stalinist "socialism in one country" worked — because it had won the war — but would also make socialism in just one country unnecessary ever again.

The Soviets proceeded to secure their East European glacis both militarily and politically. They had conquered the area with conventional military force, and they moved their military border to the limit of the Red Army's advance and continued to occupy the intervening space. This was partly to deter attack and intimidation from the West. But Soviet thinking is preeminently political-military, and it integrates the military and political aspects of power better than ours does. The Soviets knew that purely military balances are by their nature subject to change. So they used their occupation to create a stable power position at the base, by effecting a revolution in every country they occupied.

What I have just said simplifies a complex history of interaction in great power diplomacy and between diplomacy and domestic politics in Europe. That was the subject of our own American revisionist debate of the 1960s on the origins of the Cold War. But I do not believe it distorts the real history. The Soviet Union's intention to underpin its military power with systemic change in large areas of Eastern Europe was clear from the beginning and throughout. The revisionists identified options that were not chosen, roads that were not taken. However, these options had to do with timing, scope, and degree, and it seems to me that the debate has left intact the basic Soviet determination to revolutionize the area.

To secure the area for good, the Soviets imposed on Eastern Europe the system that lay at hand. This was Stalinism, the system of governance Stalin had put together in the USSR in the 1930s at such gigantic cost and with such gigantic results. It was fashioned of Russian materials. Russia too was a peasant country, it too had a tradition of

autocratic rule through bureaucracies, and Stalin manufactured a whole new elite out of peasant material to rule
bureaucratically, albeit with unprecedented force and
coherence. He created a dictatorship of party/state organs
that aspired to direct, control, and dominate every aspect of
political, economic, social, and cultural life from a single
center, and sometimes succeeded. And it was this Stalinist
system that he fastened on Eastern Europe in order to
make Soviet power last forever.

It became apparent only later that in Eastern Europe
the system was in fact a hybrid, as it included materials
that Russia and the countries of the area shared. At the
time it looked totally alien, and it was hated. It was home-
grown in the USSR, where it had won a war, but in Eastern
Europe it was imposed as a result of conquest and occupation by the Red Army, the NKVD, and hordes of other
Soviet advisors, with handfuls of local Communist stooges
providing wholly inadequate national political cover for
the operation.

The Soviets and their Communist camp followers tried
to sell this Stalinist system to the local elites and populations as top-of-the-line modernization. The promise was to
bring industry and social justice together and quickly, and
thereby to lift each country forever out of the backwardness, weakness, and dependence that had been its historic
destiny. Like the Soviet economy, the Stalinist economies of
Eastern Europe were geared for heavy industry along
traditional nineteenth- and early twentieth-century lines:
coal, iron, steel, later petrochemicals. Such industrialization, sponsored and driven by a vastly expanded and

centralized bureaucracy, was indeed one dream of the area's traditional elites. Its vehicle was the concentrated state power needed to implement a nineteenth-century ideology of economic development and national strength. Elites in these countries had never had that kind of power before for any purpose, and once they were given access to it they learned to appreciate it.

But in return, and as part of the package, politics as such were simply abolished and replaced by economics. In our liberal democracies we have economic *issues*, and they sometimes dominate the political agenda. But the political agenda itself is broad; it is whatever society comes up with, and economic issues are only one potential component. By contrast, under Stalinism *everything* was politicized, but national agendas were confined by force to economics. Legitimate domestic debate was limited to the production issues that filled the newspapers with plan fulfillment statistics and with heroic lathe and tractor operators. Politics in our sense, as a competition of interests under agreed rules and with indeterminate outcomes, was eliminated.

Another part of the Stalinist recipe was that each East European nation was tied separately and bilaterally to the USSR. The foreign relations of each country were mainly with Moscow. The Soviet military presence was secured by bilateral agreements both before and after the Warsaw Treaty Organization was invented as a pendant to NATO in the mid-1950s. The Council on Mutual Economic Assistance (CMEA, or Comecon) was invented earlier and revivified in the mid-1950s as well, but it was never more than a pale shadow of the emerging European Economic Communities. Foreign economic relations in the East were basically between each country and the USSR. Economically, the "bloc" has been aptly described as a wheel with very thick spokes and practically no rim. And this was true in most other spheres of life as well.

Still, this relentless bilateralism kept the national framework of each country in place. Each regime proclaimed itself the fulfillment of all that was best and most progressive in each nation's history. Unlike Stalin, moreover, the East European party regimes did not biologically replace the humanistic intellectuals who were the traditional carriers of national values. As in the USSR, the intelligentsia remained one of the three recognized corps in Stalinist society, along with the workers and peasants; but in contrast to the USSR, the old intelligentsia also survived physically in Eastern Europe. It was pruned where necessary, and sometimes bloodily. But the strategic thrust was to reshape it by adding masses of workers' and peasants' children to it through the vastly expanded educational systems, by making political loyalty the primary criterion for social status, and by creating a new environment where loyalty would be in the intelligentsia's self-interest.

Still, it was clear that it would take time to create the new self-interest, so in the meantime the new environment had to be imposed. And imposed it was, by the Soviets and local stooges who were often from despised national minorities to boot. It was imposed by terror, often bloody, over a third of Europe, on a hundred million people, in minute and mainly uniform detail. At the time the national form looked insignificant; the Stalinist content looked overwhelming. And to the populations who saw only harsh, alien rule, Stalinism was advertised not only as escape from their old historic destiny but as their *new* historic destiny. They were told that whether they liked it or not there was no escape, and that they had to submit, if not for their sakes, then for their family's sake, for their children.

What we in the West saw was a combined military and systemic threat from Europe's eastern half. We saw the Red Army poised to strike to the channel, and behind it and under it we saw a tyrannical system that was inimical not just to the liberty and prosperity of the East Europeans but also to ours. In our democratic thinking liberty and prosperity are functionally interrelated. They support and depend on each other. So what we saw was a total threat.

We did not respond with a total defense. We avoided the garrison state. But the West under American leadership did respond in the late 1940s and 1950s, and it responded to both parts of the threat. On the military side it built up an elaborate system of deterrence, of forces, structures, and doctrines intended to convince the Soviets that attack would not be worth the cost. In this effort and in the system it produced the United States had the lead, as the West's preeminent military power, and especially as its leading nuclear power. Since U.S. thinking tended to separate the military and political aspects of power and resented permanent mobilization as unnatural, Americans tended to focus on the military threat, and they tended to demonize the Soviets for forcing a monstrous new military burden on them.

This American military preeminence also related well to the other, systemic side of the Western response to the division of Europe by Stalinism. The military buildup protected and was eventually matched by the restoration of Western Europe on the basis of liberal democracy in politics and mixed free-market/welfare state economies. The political purpose was to make Western Europe immune to Stalinism, just as NATO and the American military commitment made it immune to the Soviet attack that would bring Stalinism in its wake. Here too, because of its economic power, the U.S. had a leading role in the beginning, with the Marshall Plan. But here, as Western Europe rebuilt, the American preoccupation with the military threat proved very tolerable to the West Europeans. In the beginning they could not afford to pay their way militarily, and they needed all their resources for economic reconstruction. The U.S. nuclear guarantee deterred the Soviets, but it was also economical to all concerned, compared to what it would have cost to match Soviet conventional superiority by conventional forces alone. Our guarantee also allowed West Germany to stay non-nuclear as it integrated into rebuilding Western Europe. And once Western Europe was rebuilt, the U.S. continued to shoulder much of the military burden, so that "little Europe," the truncated Europe of the West, continued to prosper.

Thus the West proved that Soviet military preponderance and the Stalinist system were *not* destiny west of the Iron Curtain. And for some years it was unwilling to accept Stalinism as destiny for East Europeans either. Although the motives for the offer were admittedly mixed, the Marshall Plan was, after all, offered to the East too, and the smaller East European countries that tentatively accepted were in the end waved off only on Stalin's orders. The early 1950s, which were the years of the massive retaliation doctrine on the military side, were also the years of rollback or liberation doctrine on the political front. We had a single vision in action for the whole continent. To the East it looked like active subversion, and given the facts of life about Stalinism, it *was* active subversion.

In principle, the Americans and the West Europeans believed then and have continued to believe ever since that liberal democracy and mixed economies with large free-market components are the proper prescription not only for themselves but also for Eastern Europe and for the USSR as well. But over the course of the 1950s the *practice* changed. There were many reasons for this. With Western rearmament after the Korean War, the military confrontation between East and West gradually stabilized. After Stalin's death in 1953, de-Stalinization made the USSR seem less threatening in general. The Soviets also took specific steps — unilateral troop reductions, the Austrian State Treaty in 1955 — to take the sting from the threat, and de-Stalinization spread to Eastern Europe.

If liberalization had been all that was going on, rollback might have continued as Western policy in practice as well as in principle. But it was not all. The pressure of Stalinism produced tremendous tension in Eastern Europe, for which the Soviet Union was correctly blamed. But relieving the tension through de-Stalinization produced East European crisis. Stalinist pressure meant closet civil war in the East European countries, but letting up on it after Stalin died produced crises, in East Germany in 1953 and on a larger scale in Poland and Hungary in 1956, that spilled over into the international system. The West had encouraged these eruptions in principle and in practice. Now it found it could do nothing practical to help when the Soviets moved to lance the boils, in Poland by a combination of military threat and judicious concessions, in East Germany and Hungary by Red Army reconquest, brute military force. The lessons were traumatic all the way around.

The Soviets were the most responsible, and they drew the most lessons. Even as Soviet tanks revved up to retake Budapest, on October 30, 1956, the Soviet government issued a declaration on the principles governing its relations with other Communist countries that was a kind of charter for national paths to socialism in Eastern Europe. And the Soviets recognized that the revolts in Poland and Hungary had been both anti-misery and anti-colonial. In response they adjusted their methods of imperial governance in the whole area. Previously Soviet rule had been politically direct and economically exploitative; the Soviet Union had sucked resources from Eastern Europe to help rebuild the ruined USSR. Now, by the mid-1950s, the Soviet economy had substantially recovered from its wartime losses, and it was starting to produce major new increments of raw materials, particularly oil. After the Khrushchev leadership gained firm political control at home beginning in 1957, it began to dismantle direct rule in the empire. The armies of advisors left, even the Red Army was withdrawn from some places, and the main burden of maintaining Soviet dominance shifted to economics.

This was, in fact, a gamble on the natural tendency of Stalinist economies to sink into the Soviet market. In Cold War conditions of isolation from the West and with Stalinist management techniques, in order to grow the industrializing East European economies needed raw material inputs and markets that were realistically available to them only in the Soviet Union. They wanted to produce heavy manufactured goods, and what they produced was second rate, unsaleable on hard-currency markets, so they could not buy the iron and oil they needed in return for what they had to sell except from the Soviets. As long as the Soviet Union was willing to furnish them stable supplies of raw materials and stable outlets for their shoddy manufactures, the bargain was likely to be irresistible to East Europeans on economic grounds alone.

This "economization" of Soviet rule took some time to put in place and was not much advertised. The Western response to 1956 is better known but was never admitted as a matter of principle, for excellent political reasons. Nevertheless it was equally substantial. After 1956 the West in practice came to accept Stalinism as destiny for the East Europeans. It stopped pushing actively to destroy it, and it turned instead to using bilateral means to encourage small incremental changes away from Stalinism at whatever pace the individual East European regimes wished and could afford to tolerate.

The military threat remained important to the West, but its focus broadened out from Europe to the planet. Warsaw Pact conventional forces in Europe were still threatening, but they were now seen mainly as a component of a global Soviet military threat. This global threat was to be deterred by an elaborate and interlocking system of bilateral and multilateral instruments, including arms control. In other words, the military threat was now part of a bigger picture, and dealing with it was a *multilateral* task. Dealing with the Stalinist system in Eastern Europe, by contrast, was to be a bilateral task for the individual Western countries. This meant in practice that East European Stalinism was still despised, but it was largely off the Western political screen until some crisis erupted and forced the West back into conclave to denounce it.

These separate Eastern and Western responses to the crises of the mid-1950s combined to produce a new modus vivendi in the Cold War. The year 1956 ushered in an "economization" of both East-West competition in Europe and East European domestic politics that lasted a whole generation, into the early 1980s.

Economism had a dynamic of its own. It produced recurrent efforts by East European countries either to escape the economic "iron ring" drawing them toward the Soviet market or to exploit it by snuggling into it. For the countries trying to escape, there were three possible routes. First, barter arrangements with the Third World might allow them to trade their industrial goods for precious raw materials without hard currency. Second, economic reform might equip them to produce more goods saleable on hard-currency markets. Third, Western credits might let them buy technology that would permit their economies to boost productivity *without* economic reform. The Soviets for their part were willing to tolerate such experiments, sometimes, to a degree, in some places. They had a modest confidence in the basic strength of the iron ring, and it now required them to subsidize Eastern Europe through favorable terms of trade. If experimentation relieved that burden without undue political consequences, the Soviets were willing to see it go forward. And this opened up a Western option for Eastern Europe. The West was now permitted to compete for influence in the area on an economic basis. This in turn depoliticized the intensely political East-West competition for influence there, and that had tremendous political advantages for all sides.

The Soviets could tell themselves that they were merely doing their fraternal duty; that they were just building the infrastructure of the "socialist community"; and that dominion was the last thing they had in mind. The U.S. could tell itself it was merely doing business, disposing of surpluses, letting its businessmen make profits; rollback or liberation was the last thing it had in mind. Of course, neither side forgot its own "last things," and each hoped the other would. But although it was a fiction, "economism" was a very convenient fiction for both superpowers.

It was also convenient to the West Europeans. The United States remained fixed on its global view of East-West relations and fascinated by their military aspect. It was willing to put great resources into globalism. The way was thus open for America's European allies to put *their* growing marginal resources, political and economic, into East-West problems in Europe. The U.S. was tolerant of these efforts. On the economic side, it recognized that it was far away — so that trade cost more — while the Europeans were neighbors. Politically, because the U.S. had such an open system, its economic relations with Communist countries were naturally going to be more politicized than Western Europe's, and thus more hedged in by and vulnerable to legislative restrictions. So the West Europeans gained a margin of maneuver, and they used it to develop and pursue individual goals across the East-West divide.

This was particularly the case with West Germany. Firmly anchored in the West, it was also part of a divided nation. The German Democratic Republic (GDR) was German, and there were substantial German minorities in Poland's ex-German territories and in Romania. The Federal Republic thus had an interest in Eastern Europe as persistent and at least as powerful as that of the United States, which saw the area as part of the global chessboard with which we also had historic and human ties. So beginning in the late 1960s, as superpower détente began and under the cover of détente, the Federal Republic developed its own Eastern policy. Using both political and economic means, it moved to stabilize its relations first with Romania, then with the USSR, then with Poland, and finally with the GDR and the rest. Because *Ostpolitik* was driven by inner-German considerations, it was allergic to crisis, for fear that crisis would produce crackdown on other Germans. Hence the West Germans tended to argue that the West should pursue a policy of all carrots and no sticks, of benefits but no sanctions, and that Europe should be insulated from downturns in other areas of East-West relations. This in turn caused friction with the U.S. and other NATO allies, and it added another set of issues to those NATO had to manage already. But that kind of friction at least proved that the Atlantic Alliance was indeed a free house with many mansions, and as long as economism and détente lasted, the costs were quite manageable.

So Cold War economism had advantages for the superpowers and the West Europeans. Still, it was above all convenient to the East Europeans. Domestically, it perpetuated the regimes' fiction that politics had actually been replaced by economics, the line that their revolutions were permanent because all political issues had been resolved. It also gave the ruling parties scope to nationalize themselves. In these years they began to compete in earnest for the national themes that were so dear to the populations and to replace the first revolutionary generation, who were looked on as Soviet stooges even when they were not of minority origin, with home-grown products of their own Communist higher education. The basic Stalinist structures — monopoly party/state decision making in industrializing economies, with everything politicized and thus no politics at all — remained in place. But there was tremendous economic growth, which made the penury and misery of high Stalinism a thing of the past and which created space for some tension-reducing experimentation.

Beyond the domestic fronts economism also had an international payoff for the countries of Eastern Europe. Except when they erupted in crisis, they were out of the international limelight. They resented their invisibility, but it also had advantages. For the Soviets the basic Stalinist system was still in place, and the iron ring still worked. But the smaller countries that were so inclined were at least able to keep the ring from getting tighter and to develop some Western ties in return for some Western access. These ties were greatly appreciated by the populations, and they were valued even by the regimes. And in the upshot a degree of genuine diversity emerged in the area, far greater than anything the Soviets had tolerated in practice, much less in principle, under high Stalinism.

However, this degree of flexibility and diversity was not enough to eliminate the occasional crisis or the constant threat of crisis. The Stalinist system was too unnatural for that. The approved metropolitan model for area conservatives was the Soviet "real socialism" of the Brezhnev years, and it was still essentially Stalinist and structurally rigid. The Soviets remained attached to their leadership of the socialist camp, and given their definition of "socialism" this meant that a crisis in one country was a still a crisis for all of them together.

The Soviets were not itching for fights in Eastern Europe, but this did not always help. In the immediate post-Stalin years domestic infighting in Moscow had distracted them, and this had allowed crises in Eastern Europe to mature, which in turn led the Soviets to crack down. The pattern was repeated in the post-Khrushchev years in

Czechoslovakia in 1968. It was not repeated everywhere. Just as Poland managed to escape 1956 with some concessions because the Red Army was busy in Hungary, Hungary managed to put some real economic reform in place in 1968 partly because the Red Army was busy in Czechoslovakia. Still, crisis *did* come in Czechoslovakia, and after much hesitation the Soviets finally responded with another military invasion. Afterward they even generalized the experience by what was known in the West as the Brezhnev Doctrine, a regressive reaffirmation of their right to intervene to save socialism in any country where they judged it was threatened and could scare up a handful of stooges to invite them in.

But these threatening or real crises did not alter the basic structure of economism in Eastern Europe and in the Cold War. Crisis was about all the West saw in Eastern Europe. The resort to military repression in Czechoslovakia refreshed Western recognition of what was called the "policing role" of Soviet conventional forces in Eastern Europe, but the West continued to deal with those forces as an aspect of the global military threat. The systemic differences were still to be handled through patient, incremental bilateralism. The Soviets permitted some bilateral transactions, but they also continued to subsidize the East European economies in the confidence that the Soviet market was their natural home, and they continued to insist that they and the East Europeans were all one big socialist family, so that what one of them did just naturally mattered a lot to the rest.

Thus, the great East-West institutional process dealing with Europe — the Conference on Security and Cooperation in Europe, or CSCE — had very little to do with Eastern Europe when it was born in these years. At the time it looked backward rather than forward. It had begun as a classic Soviet peace initiative of the 1950s, and it resurfaced in 1969 as an Eastern way of reducing the political costs of the invasion of Czechoslovakia. The East then used CSCE to seek Western ratification of the postwar territorial settlement. The West used it as a bargaining chip for a Berlin settlement and for negotiations on Mutual and Balanced Force Reductions, or MBFR, which were designed to relieve Vietnam-era U.S. domestic pressure for bringing U.S. forces home from Europe. Once CSCE negotiations got underway, the West developed their human rights aspect, but this was less in order to deal with systemic differences in Europe than to gain the support of domestic political constituencies. The Soviets detested this aspect as interference in Communist domestic affairs, but they remained hooked on what was after all their own initiative. At Helsinki in 1975, thirty-five countries of North America and Europe — all of them except Albania — reconciled these competing priorities enough to sign a Final Act that registered commitments in three so-called baskets, security, economic relations, and human rights and contacts, and they promised to continue. The Final Act was indeed a promising framework, and the process went on and developed a life of its own. The East Europeans helped create CSCE, they loved it, and they used it to multiply their bilateral ties with their Western CSCE partners. But CSCE was also an intricate process, a diplomat's dream but a political leader's bargaining chip. It scarcely looked like a vehicle pointed toward the future, and it was not mainly about Eastern Europe.

So CSCE was not the central focus even for the East Europeans. What preoccupied them at the end of the 1970s was rather the agony of the whole economistic system. Economism as such had never been defined and accepted for what it was, and it was a loose thing; its various parts prospered or rotted in dispersed order. But now it was rotting in every part.

Within Eastern Europe Stalinism was running out of steam as a system of economic management. The problem was defined rather chastely as the need to move from extensive to intensive economic development in order to capture the benefits of the scientific-technological revolution. The truth was more drastic: The whole system was degenerating. This was also occurring in the Soviet Union, but there the size of the economy masked it, for a while. In the smaller East European economies, however, it was visible everywhere: slowing growth rates, sagging living standards, multiplying bottlenecks, accelerating if hidden inflation. In country after country Stalinism was performing less and less well against its own standards.

The economic basis for *international* economism was also eroding away. Two oil shocks in a decade shriveled the marginal resources the West used to compete for influence in Eastern Europe. Western economic anemia in turn shrank the markets the East Europeans needed to earn the hard currency to pay for quality imports or to service debt. Western businessmen and bankers discovered not only that business was vulnerable to politics — Western sanctions or Eastern extortion on political grounds — but that even at best, state-trading countries are difficult partners to work with. Profits are hard to come by, and modest when they come. Many East European countries were having trouble paying their debts and were reducing Western purchases in order to use hard currency earnings to manage their debt problems. After the Soviet invasion of reforming Czechoslovakia discredited economic reform politically, in the 1970s Western trade and credits had become Eastern Europe's line of best resistance to the iron ring of rising dependence on the Soviet market. By mid-decade Western trade and credits began to falter and then to dry up.

Meanwhile the Soviets were also becoming more demanding. They were still willing to supply raw materials in return for East European manufactures, but the costs of producing their raw materials were rising astronomically, and they were becoming more cost-conscious. Their own Western markets were shrinking too, and they increasingly preferred to send their raw materials West for hard currency and high technology rather than to Eastern Europe. For what they still supplied their CMEA partners, they wanted better goods, precisely those goods that the East Europeans could most easily sell on hard-currency markets. So the economic iron ring was simultaneously getting both tighter and more costly to maintain at all.

With growth rates and living standards wobbling, with the West unwilling to play the economic game, and with the Soviet Union playing it harder, the East Europeans were threatened once again with *politics*. But in politics they — and their neighbors East and West — saw only peril. This is because in the meantime they had become more diverse, the regimes had nationalized themselves, and the peculiar course of their domestic development under Stalinism assured that a return to politics meant redoubled nationalism.

The reasons why were not straightforward. They resulted as much from developments under socialism as from the continued vitality of pre-socialist values. The educational revolution all these countries had been through meant a vastly expanded intelligentsia in each of them. But the intelligentsia now went far beyond the old humanistic intellectuals who had been the traditional spokesmen for national values. Industrialization had added a huge new group of technically trained intellectuals that threatened to swamp the humanists. Meanwhile, industrialization and education together had also expanded not just the working class in general but skilled workers in particular. By the 1970s, however, economic growth was slowing, and this narrowed opportunities for upward social mobility, opportunities to escape the working class through education. University slots increasingly went to the children of the elite who had made it through the first time round. So the aspirations of both the humanists and the skilled workers were now threatened. Together — if they could get together — they constituted a potential constellation of purveyors and consumers of nationalism on a new scale. Both groups were larger than ever before, and both were more discontent than at any time since the war. The danger was greatest in the more developed countries, but in systemic terms it was a danger for everyone.

The East European regimes were acutely conscious of all these developments, but they could not say so; indeed, they had every reason to deny they were taking place at all. They therefore clung to economism at home and abroad as to the ark of the covenant. They insisted that economics was the real issue and that talk of human rights was merely illegitimate interference in internal affairs. They invented ever more urgent expedients to keep growth going; to cadge favors from the Soviets, or from the West; to curry favor with their populations, or to repress them. The West for its part was usually oblivious, and when not oblivious then indifferent in the absence of a crisis. It was preoccupied with its own economic troubles, with the disintegration of détente, with the fate of arms control. And with Brezhnev's decline, the Soviets were still wary, and even dangerous, but they were also inward-looking and distracted.

Once again it was a crisis that brought all these problems into political focus. The Gierek regime in Poland had come to power in 1970 after a workers' revolt. Throughout the 1970s it was the area's most vocal practitioner of "goulash communism" at home and of going West for credits to import technology that would boost productivity and then living standards, but without economic reform. Beginning in 1976 it foundered, and its dissolution produced a full-scale national crisis in 1980-81. Internationally the Polish crisis was enveloped in the decline of détente. It therefore made the West Europeans more restless with U.S. leadership, made European détente for the Europeans more attractive. But it did not alter the familiar prescription: arms control for the military threat, slow bilateralism for the systemic differences. In Eastern Europe, however, the Polish crisis was the real writing on the wall. Solidarity was precisely the coalition that was the political nightmare of every regime, a coalition of skilled workers and humanistic intellectuals that spoke, however carefully, in the name of repressed national values. However special the Polish road to socialism was, however specific Polish conditions were, Poland too was still a Stalinist system. So they were all on the line.

The Soviets were preoccupied with their own succession struggle, and for them the Polish crisis was difficult but not yet really problematic. As the old Viennese saying went, it was desperate but not yet serious. When Polish rather than Soviet soldiers did the dirty work in December 1981, the Soviets were rather proud of their restraint, but this did not mask their satisfaction with the classic if unwelcome solution of another military crackdown. The Polish crisis became problematic for the Soviets only *after* the solution, when they realized the solution had not worked. By that time, however, they were ready to define the problem in other than classic terms.

But that is to leap ahead. At the turn of the 1980s the economistic structure that had seen East European politics and East-West competition in Europe through a whole generation was a rotting hulk. It was still afloat, but it was dead in the water. Most people did not understand this, and those who did were keeping quiet about it. That was not entirely a bad thing. In politics sudden shocks and shifts can be dangerous, and belief in the old can help responsible statesmen muddle through to the new on their own terms. But the question for us is whether the East Europeans and their neighbors could begin to fashion new solutions to the increasingly urgent and increasingly political problems before them all, and a new structure for dealing with them. The answer lies in the story of the 1980s.

Chapter 6

Slouching towards Bethlehem: The Division of Europe in the 1980s

Like the story of superpower relations in the 1980s, the evolution of the division of Europe as an international problem over the course of the decade is a story of countries doing what they did — even good things, even the right thing — for their own reasons — even the wrong reasons, and in any case political reasons — step by painful step.

Here the East European regimes had a bigger role to play from the beginning, and they were eager to play it. But they were also eager to keep that role mainly supportive and to define it mainly in terms of economics. The Polish crisis of 1980-81 showed them all not only what was wrong with the past but what was wrong with the future. The Gierek regime in Poland had been economistic par excellence in both domestic and international politics, and the rise of Solidarity on the ruins of economism was a warning throughout the area. When the Polish army cracked down under martial law in December 1981, all the regimes breathed a sigh of relief. But this time the classic solution of a military crackdown did not work.

The most important reasons why it did not work were the courage and fortitude of the Solidarity coalition of workers and intellectuals and Solidarity's fidelity to what it had learned before it was repressed. It represented national values, but in Poland these included democratic and religious values as well as raw nationalism, and Solidarity kept promoting them when it was driven underground. There it kept its structure in place, it maintained its Western support, and it kept insisting that for economic reform to work the Polish working class had to be in at the take-off and that political reform was needed to put it and keep it there. Meanwhile the martial law regime kept consumption up in order to reduce the cost of repression and make it stick. But this proved an intolerable burden on the already exhausted Stalinist management system. Without Western ties, with the huge hard-currency debt spiraling upward, and with the West demanding political rollback, any hope of digging out by Stalinist means alone, even slowly and patiently, gradually died away.

Having seen the writing on the wall, the other East European regimes responded in diverse ways. The Romanian response was the most vigorous. Nicolae Ceausescu had already co-opted nationalism in the 1960s and 1970s, and Romania did not have the intelligentsia tradition of some Slavic countries, the tradition that the intelligentsia as a self-conscious "government of souls" set over against the regime. So keeping intellectuals and workers apart took less effort in Romania than elsewhere. Now, in the 1980s, as Ceausescu became more and more bearish about the advantages of Western economic ties, he embarked on a full-scale campaign to pay off Romania's substantial hard-currency debt under the banner of restoring national independence. This crippled the economy, led to further repression, and sacrificed most of Romania's Western ties. But it seemed to him worth the cost. If the American motto was a Europe "whole and free," as Vice President Bush suggested at Vienna in September 1983 (long before he took it up again as President in 1989), Ceausescu's was a Romania "Stalinist, poor and independent."

But Ceausescu's response was also extreme compared to the rest of the area. The other regimes chose basically to stand pat where they were before, making small adjustments to defend what they had or seizing marginal new opportunities. Bulgaria, for instance, took advantage of its relative isolation in these years to officially abolish its Turkish minority through forced assimilation. It was suspected by the West of conniving in the assassination attempt on the Pope, and it was less beloved even by the Soviets partly for that reason. So the regime probably calculated that it had little to lose by trying to impose ethnic homogeneity. In general, however, such adventures were few and far between. Continuity was the rule.

But this in turn meant that the genuine diversification which had taken place in Eastern Europe under late Stalinism accelerated at the margin. The effects were both domestic and international. Most of the regimes denied the need for any structural change, but they all wanted to keep ahead of the nationalist wave they now saw gathering force. So throughout the area in the late 1970s and early 1980s, there was a reawakening of national political cultures and national political problematics. The regimes had always tried to co-opt nationalism, and now they tried harder. But it was harder than ever to do, and this led them to tug at the traces both in their relations with each other and in relations with the Soviets and the West.

Traditional national issues now floated up to the surface of East European intra-state relations and occasionally popped out in public dispute. As Romanian repression deepened, the Transylvanian issue between Hungary and Romania sharpened again, and the Hungarian regime felt forced to respond more and more forthrightly to indignation from below at home. Still, like Macedonia and Bessarabia, Transylvania was a southeast European issue, far from the main arena of East-West confrontation in Central Europe. But even in Central Europe such issues were appearing or reappearing, the more ominous for their location and the players involved. The "blank spots" in Polish-Soviet history, such as responsibility for the Katyn massacre of 1940, surfaced as an issue; there was a Polish-GDR dispute over maritime boundaries; and especially, there was another round in the continuing struggle between Poland and the GDR for Soviet and Western favor.

Much of the substance in international relations *within* the socialist camp had involved fierce competition between these two northern countries for the status of the Soviet Union's best friend in the area. Each had assets and disabilities. Poland had its size and its attraction for Westerners, but it seemed always on the brink of economic and political turbulence. The GDR had its economic strength and efficiency, its special ties with the Federal Republic, and the bulk of Soviet forces stationed in Europe. But it also had its special political weakness, which required sympathetic attention. The Soviet Union had traditionally kept Poland and the GDR both loyal by playing them off against each other. Now, however, Poland was an economic and political basket case and almost off the international chessboard. Into this vacuum both the GDR and Hungary sought to move, the GDR by developing its West German ties, the Hungarians by competing for Poland's old role as the West's favorite bridge to the East.

Hungary's effort was tolerable to all concerned. Hungary had introduced some real economic reform in the 1960s and had kept it alive in the 1970s, so everyone understood that it was the East European economy most dependent on Western ties. The Kádár regime had taken the cutting edge off traditional Hungarian nationalism and made it run in harness with other national values. Hence noises from Hungary about détente for the Europeans were not surprising, and even noises about the special role of small countries in keeping détente going were not thought dangerous. But when the *GDR* joined Hungary in touting a small-nation role, and then began to talk about *German* détente for Germans and about the special need to keep war from breaking out again on German soil, the international system, even including the distracted Soviets, began to take notice.

Still, East European tugging at the traces was not by it-self enough to jar the international shape of the division of Europe. For that to happen, this bickering and restlessness first had to spill over into the main ring, into the issues that the West and the Soviet Union defined as important. And in the early 1980s that had to mean military security and arms control.

After 1956 there had been tacit Soviet-Western agree-ment that military security was the "core issue." There was indeed a framework for multilateral work on some of the systemic differences that lay behind the military security problem in the CSCE process that continued after the Hel-sinki Final Act was signed in 1975. But although CSCE was precious to the East Europeans, it was of secondary impor-tance to the West. The main thrust of Western policy was for individual countries to develop bilateral ties — economic, cultural, scientific, political — that would al-leviate by small steps the consequences of the division of Europe. At the turn of the 1980s, Western attention was riveted on the decline of détente and the degeneration of its arms-control component.

And the death of détente produced tension within the Western alliance on both the military and the systemic sides of the problem of Europe's division. Informally for a generation, formally since the mid-1970s, the U.S. approach was to pursue better bilateral relations with those East European countries that showed some foreign policy inde-pendence or some domestic liberalism, and that thereby differentiated themselves from the Soviets. But the Reagan Administration's comprehensive and ideological view of the East-West competition tended to lump all these countries together with the Soviets, and it tended to see East-West ties in Europe mainly as candidates for punitive action in the global struggle, as if they were without merit of their own that was worth saving. At the same time, the Administration was intent on reaffirming American leadership of the West, and it therefore wanted its European allies to take the same view or to act as if they did. For instance, in 1981 it suggested linking resumption of strategic arms talks to the course of Polish events, and then, when Polish martial law was declared in December of that year, it wanted East-West bilateral ties cut as sanctions. And here the Europeans resisted.

It was therefore the Polish crisis that brought matters to a head in the West, as it was bringing them to a head in the East. The U.S. was determined to impose sanctions on both the Poles and the Soviets, but because it wished to avoid a repeat of the Carter Administration's experience with NATO disarray after the Soviet invasion of Afghanistan in 1979, it was also determined to lead the West from the beginning. The allies for their part were not averse to U.S. leadership, but they also wanted to avoid irreparable damage to the texture of East-West ties in Europe. The issue was joined in the urgent NATO consultations of January 1982, and the result was a compromise. The allies agreed to sanctions, but they insisted that sanctions be reversible provided the Polish regime fulfilled three tough conditions: an end to martial law, release of political prisoners, and genuine dialogue with the Church and Solidarity. At the time this looked as much like pie in the sky as the zero option in INF. But conditional reversibility also meant that there was now a way forward — even if it only led back to the status quo ante — and that this was now the policy of the whole Western alliance.

Moreover, the U.S. desire to assert leadership rather than act unilaterally in this deteriorating situation also led to the American discovery of the Helsinki Final Act. If the West Europeans were to be brought along, it was important to have some general reason beyond immediate outrage for punishing and pillorying the Soviets and the offending East Europeans. The Final Act and the process that had emerged from it were something everyone had signed on to, East and West. So it was CSCE that was chosen to justify the Western sanctions. But even if it functioned as a stick in circumstances of 1982, once the United States was attached to it, CSCE became available for other purposes as well.

This was because CSCE combined security and human rights — the military and systemic aspects of the European problem. The Final Act itself was a diplomatic trade-off of the two: The West made commitments concerning the postwar territorial status quo in return for Eastern commitments on human rights and contacts. In conditions of disintegrating détente, however, this framework had active appeal for East and West Europeans alike. It provided both with ways to insulate intra-European ties from the vagaries of superpower relations. For East Europeans it was a part of the status quo to which they were attached. And for West Europeans it was a means of asserting their special regional interest in the military security and arms-control issues that the two superpowers commonly negotiated between themselves.

Already in 1978 the French had proposed negotiations within the CSCE context on conventional arms control from the Atlantic to the Urals. The East had counterproposed two-stage negotiations, first on confidence-building measures concerning mechanisms for notification and inspection of force movements and then on actual reductions in forces. For the time being the only outcome was a CSCE negotiation on certain confidence-building measures. Negotiation on actual reductions remained in the MBFR talks that had been going on in Vienna since 1973. MBFR was limited to a narrow Central European zone, the French did not participate in the talks, and they had also produced no result. So the Europeans wanted to breathe new life into the CSCE security basket, largely because they wanted some additional leverage on military issues affecting their vital interests.

Of course, the Europeans had a good deal of say in the "battle for Europe" that continued over INF. U.S. Euromissile deployments in late 1983 were a victory, but the Soviets continued the battle even after they walked out of both INF and START and followed up with counter-deployments. Political blood continued to flow in the form of a higher level of opposition to nuclear weapons as such throughout Europe; of leftward shifts in the opposition parties of two major allied countries, Britain and the FRG; and of shaken confidence in U.S. leadership and in the value to Europe of the whole Western system of extended deterrence. It took only relatively minor policy adjustments to keep the system itself in place, but the system as such was weakened. The Western nuclear debate continued after 1983, and it was this debate, and then steps the East took to keep it going, that made things happen on the problems of Europe's division.

The battle for Europe had been fought on the nuclear issue, and as the nuclear debate continued the Atlantic countries began to recall why it was that they had put nuclear weapons in Europe in the first place. Nuclear weapons were there, after all, because they were an economical way of deterring the tremendous Soviet conventional military threat on the continent, for Western countries that wished first to recover and then to prosper. If we wanted to raise rather than lower the nuclear threshold, the threshold in a conflict where Soviet conventional advantage might force us to use nuclear weapons, then either that Soviet advantage would have to be reduced or the Western conventional deterrent would have to be built up. It was clear that the buildup option would be tremendously expensive, because conventional forces are so much more expensive than nuclear weapons, and no one wanted to pay. So while the main political focus stayed on nuclear weapons, slowly another part of the fundamental problem began to emerge and come back into focus. That part was disproportionate Soviet conventional military power in the center of Europe, and it raised the question of why the Soviets had put so many soldiers and so much hardware on the Elbe River line.

Still, there was little reason to expect that the Soviets and East Europeans would take the point and begin to deal with their *systems* rather than just the armaments needed to maintain them. In 1983 only the Poles were playing. In December 1982 President Reagan had announced that the United States would respond positively if the Polish government introduced meaningful liberalization measures, and he repeated it in May and June 1983. In June Pope John Paul II had a second successful visit to his homeland, and over the course of the year the regime released most of its political prisoners. In response, we reversed some of our sanctions, with small steps on debt, fishing, and aviation. With Romania we also showed the sliding scale could go the other way, that sanctions could be applied as well as lifted depending on East European behavior, when in March 1983 we threatened to rescind most-favored-nation tariff treatment until the Romanian government assured us it would not implement a 1982 decree charging emigrants for the cost of their education.

Vice President Bush's support for making Europe whole again in Vienna that September followed a visit to two Warsaw Pact countries, and in the same speech he also reaffirmed the differentiation policy with which we pursued that goal vis-à-vis Eastern Europe. But only the Poles were willing to test U.S. willingness to move forward and not just backward in bilateral relations. The second half of 1984 was marked by more prisoner releases, and again we responded, this time by restoring scientific exchanges and lifting our veto on Polish membership in the International Monetary Fund. But it was small potatoes and few in a hill. Western attention remained concentrated on nuclear issues, and when it strayed beyond them to the conventional arms field, it focused on chemical weapons rather than troops, with the U.S. proposal of April 1984 to ban production and stocking on a global basis. This proposal had a future, but at the time it still looked backward rather than forward: It was basically another big, ambitious proposal from the Reagan Administration that was intended primarily to challenge and punish the Soviets. In this case the target was yellow rain, the poisonous agents they were alleged to have made available for use in third-area situations.

Now, however, the Soviet policy engine started to turn again. By mid-1984 a leadership holding pattern had been worked out between Chernenko and Gorbachev, and things began to move. That summer and fall saw the first tentative Soviet steps away from the post-deployment freeze, and after Reagan's reelection in November agreement was quickly reached to return to superpower nuclear arms control. Most of the movement was, in fact, in superpower relations. But elements of Soviet European policy also showed signs of renewed life. Earlier in the year the Soviets had faced unusual public backlash about their INF counterdeployments in both Czechoslovakia and the GDR. They had gone ahead anyway. Now, in September, after repeated failed hints, they waved two East European leaders, Todor Zhivkov of Bulgaria and Erich Honecker of the GDR, off scheduled trips to West Germany. If the Soviets were returning to foreign policy, then, they seemed to be reaffirming their traditional ways: superpower negotiations, a lighter rein for Poland, a tighter rein for the GDR.

For the first year or so after Gorbachev became General Secretary in March 1985, the Soviets stuck very much to traditional ways. The new leadership's focus was on personnel and beyond that on the economy; in foreign policy, it concentrated on superpower relations, and especially on nuclear arms control and SDI, in the run-up to the Geneva Summit that November. It was not eager to spread its policy wings and thereby alienate traditionalists. This was also true regarding Eastern Europe, where 1985 was a tentative year of watchful waiting. Even the activist Poles drew back: Released political prisoners were rearrested, and relations with the West suffered accordingly. After all, the Soviets were as attached as the East Europeans were to the thesis that the real problems in Eastern Europe were economic rather than political. They were as unlikely as the East Europeans were to depart from proven paths until they were forced to do so by their own political dynamic. At the end of the year, in fact, the West had the initiative when it came to conventional arms control, with a new MBFR proposal tabled in December.

But by this time the Soviet political dynamic called for broad-gauge, bold, visionary foreign policy programs. The new leadership's effort to build broader personnel support was proceeding, but it was not moving fast. It was proving hard to tinker out Soviet economic reform. And political reform was the last thing people wanted to think about. Foreign policy was thus a natural makeweight. But it was also not easy to make specific moves in foreign policy, and Gorbachev turned to bold vision instead. Given Soviet attachment to nuclear issues, the vision naturally focussed first on nuclear weapons, in the program to eliminate them by the year 2000 that he launched in January 1986. But once he was on the visionary track, the logical next focus was conventional armaments in Europe. So in April in East Berlin he proposed very substantial, equal NATO and Warsaw Pact reductions in all components of land and tactical air forces, including both conventional and tactical nuclear weapons, from the Atlantic to the Urals.

For the time being the impact on the West was fairly small. In the short term NATO responded at Halifax in May with a statement saying it too cared about conventional arms control and would study the issues. When they met in Budapest in June, the Warsaw Pact foreign ministers turned Gorbachev's concept into an appeal on behalf of the whole Pact. The Eastern proposals now accepted in principle the long-standing Western demand for on-site inspection to monitor agreements and the Atlantic-to-the-Urals area the French had first demanded in 1978. This produced early results in the CSCE negotiations on confidence-building measures that were going on in Stockholm. In September 1986 the talks there concluded successfully with ground-breaking new agreements on challenge inspections. And in December in Brussels, NATO finally floated its own program on conventional arms control. It insisted on the asymmetries and disparities in the European balance, and to deal with them it proposed East-West discussion of a whole new mandate for negotiations covering all of Europe.

The general effect of this 1986 to-and-fro on conventional arms in Europe was greater than the specific. The exchanges moved the military security problem on the divided continent higher up the international agenda, and they ensured that the allies of the two superpowers would be involved from the ground up in negotiations. But even this general effect could not have produced forward movement on conventional issues without the jolt of the superpower summit in Reykjavik. Buried in the high drama of near-success and final failure over strategic and space arms was a breakthrough on INF affecting Europe. Reykjavik produced agreement that each side would have only one hundred long-range intermediate-range warheads, all outside Europe. It was true that in the immediate aftermath of the summit the Soviets relinked actual signing of this INF agreement to conclusion of agreements on START and space as well. But the handwriting was on the wall: The INF zero option, for Europe at least, was within reach. And this posed the political question of the next step — which had to be on the conventional side — in the sharpest possible terms.

For the Soviets the answer to that question was both very easy and very difficult. It was very easy for them to push their denuclearization campaign. This was, after all, in their blueprint, the January 1986 program. Tactically, it kept nuclear issues front and center in public opinion and thereby helped to weaken West European confidence in the American deterrent and to divide NATO. In other words, it gave them a way to continue fighting the battle for Europe through the back door. But the longer that battle went on, the more the West Europeans began to ask again why the West had nuclear weapons in the first place, and to answer again that they were, after all, a relatively cheap way of deterring an overwhelming Soviet conventional military threat. The political logic of the battle thus brought the Soviets face to face with the issue of why they needed so much force in Central Europe. To argue credibly for denuclearization, they needed to do something about their conventional force superiority. And this led back to the systemic differences, the fragile Stalinist dictatorships that their forces had been put in place to defend.

Still, even this would not have been enough without a dynamic impulse from the heart of Soviet politics. It is true that after two years in place the Gorbachev leadership finally began in April 1987 to grapple seriously with the problems of the empire. The United States had meanwhile activated its own approach to Eastern Europe. In a series of visits to the area by Deputy Secretary of State John Whitehead beginning in late 1986, the U.S. developed and presented new challenge programs for relations with every country. In response to a final Polish amnesty for political prisoners in September, President Reagan lifted remaining U.S. sanctions on Poland in February 1987. That September the Vice President visited Poland and told State Council Chairman Wojciech Jaruzelski that if political reform and national reconciliation continued, the U.S. would respond in the economic field. But it was not this modest U.S. challenge that stirred the Soviets to action. The U.S. approach, after all, held out the promise of renewed East European economic relations with the West, and that was not unattractive to the Soviets at a time when they were increasingly conscious of the cost to them of subsidizing derelict East

European economies. What moved them was not the United States but their own policy imperatives.

When the Soviets finally announced a revamped approach to Eastern Europe in speeches by Gorbachev in Prague and by Ligachev in Budapest in April 1987, it appeared that those imperatives led in contradictory directions. Some of the new approach was new, but most of it was old. The main point of Gorbachev's speech had to do with denuclearization rather than Eastern Europe: It was in Prague that he proposed the so-called second zero, elimination of nuclear missiles in the range between battlefield weapons and those to be renounced under INF. When he and Ligachev did address Eastern Europe, they said in effect that the Soviets wanted higher-quality economic goods from each country, but that they would leave it up to the individual countries to determine what political and economic mechanisms would be required to produce those goods. This was indeed a license for more diversity, but it was also Khrushchevian economism revisited. It meant a continued Soviet gamble that the East European leaderships still needed the Soviet economy whatever they did with the West, and whatever reforms they introduced at home. The Soviets had been blamed for the crises of 1956, and the Khrushchev leadership had introduced economism to prevent new ones. Now Gorbachev was reaffirming economism before any new crisis broke out. If and when crisis came, the Soviets clearly hoped, the finger of blame would point squarely inward at the East Europeans and not east toward Moscow.

So even foreign policy dynamics were not enough to produce a genuinely new Soviet approach. In the end it took Soviet domestic politics to unlock the door. In 1987 it became apparent that domestic economic reform was politically stymied; and Gorbachev turned to politics to mobilize mass support for reform and lay the groundwork for getting the personnel support that economic reform needed to move on. This turn from economic to political reform was new, and it came with a political price tag: political tension rising into the highest levels of the leadership. Despite or because of this tension (we do not know what trade-offs were involved), the whole leadership decided as a matter of principle and policy that the economic reform they all supported was not going to be feasible unless it was accompanied and underpinned by major political reform.

Now, the objective of the Gorbachev leadership was to save socialism by making it work, and the Soviets were attached to its leadership of the socialist camp. So beginning in 1987 they licensed adoption of the same formula in Eastern Europe. To be sure, they were determined not to impose their formula directly, if only to avoid the onus of blame for explosions. But just adopting the formula in the Soviet Union had potentially dramatic consequences for the rest of the empire.

This was because the new Soviet line set orthodoxy adrift in each East European country. Always before, whatever the Soviets called "socialist" had been defined as efficient; now the Soviets were saying that practical efficiency, how things actually worked, would be the criterion for viable socialism. This in turn removed the fixed Soviet reference point for domestic debate on what was efficient and what needed to be conserved. Indeed, to the extent the Soviet Union was still a model, it was becoming a model for the political reform needed to make economic reform work; for *glasnost*; for democratization; for legitimate public roles for intellectuals and for hitherto repressed groups, including national groups; for experimentation with new forms of public debate and political action. To the extent that late Stalinism was no longer a model, its inefficiencies and tyrannies became all the harder to justify, and they had to be justified increasingly on grounds of national specifics.

Beginning in 1987, the result was acceleration and consolidation of diversity in Eastern Europe and invigoration of its national base in each country. And although bickering among the East European governments also increased, as between Hungary and Romania over Transylvania, the effect was now primarily in domestic rather than foreign affairs. Driven by their own dynamics, Poland and Hungary espoused the new Soviet formula with enthusiasm. It provided socialist cover and potential support from both the Soviets and the West for the economic and political experimentation they felt they needed to begin the long road to economic recovery. Bulgaria and Czechoslovakia had very long historical shadows to jump over — their leaders had been in power since 1954 and 1968, respectively, so it was hard to place blame for past mistakes safely. These two countries thus gave lip service to the new formula but basically sought to limit reform to the economic sphere. The

GDR and Romania, for their part, denied the need for any reform at all and paid a price. The GDR was rich by Eastern standards, and the regime could afford concessions to its population regarding travel to the West and religious practice. These kept GDR ties to the FRG alive and allowed the regime to deny there was a problem. The price it paid was to watch Poland pass it on the rail to become once again the Soviet Union's favorite area ally and the apple of Western eyes on Eastern Europe. By contrast, Romania was poor even by Eastern standards, and Ceausescu turned up the pressure on his population and made the country a pariah not only with the West but with other socialist countries as well. My name is SeeMore=See more butts

In practical terms the Soviet Union now tailored its own relations with the countries of the area according to how they performed against its own formula requiring political reform to make economic reform work. In principle the West had always viewed the problem in just that way. It had believed from the beginning that Stalinism was not only tyrannical but had to be inefficient; that economic efficiency required the market; that the market required some liberty to make it work; and that movement in Eastern Europe toward greater democracy and pluralism in politics and toward more market-oriented economic management was going to be required if the consequences of the division of Europe were ever to be overcome and the division itself eliminated. That was the principle which had underlain the U.S. policy of differentiation and which now underlay the U.S. challenge programs for bilateral relations with each country. Those relations now began to develop in a way that put Poland and Hungary, the political reformers, at the top of the differentiation ladder; Bulgaria, Czechoslovakia and the GDR in the middle; and Romania at the very bottom. And coming from its different direction, this was precisely where the Soviet Union ended up too.

But one more step was required before ending the division of Europe could emerge as the great, common East-West goal of early 1989. Here too the Reagan-Gorbachev meeting at Reykjavik provided the catalyst. The progress on nuclear arms control that Reykjavik registered and pushed forward forced the problem of the European conventional imbalance willy-nilly up the international agenda. But the spectacle of Reagan and Gorbachev negotiating the fate of deterrence by themselves brought all the West European restlessness with American leadership to a sharp boil. Gorbachev had turned up the heat even further in April 1987 when he proposed the "second zero" for nuclear weapons between battlefield and INF range. NATO had no such weapons and bought on to the proposal in June. It was incorporated into the INF Treaty signed at the Washington Summit in December. But Western conservatives were sickened by the pace of denuclearization, and they reacted, but in diverging ways. In Europe and especially in the Federal Republic, many conservatives fled forward and joined the Left in pressing for the "third zero" that Gorbachev now duly proposed, the elimination of battlefield weapons. This would mean the elimination of all U.S. land-based nuclear systems from the continent, and it would limit the U.S. nuclear deterrent to what the U.S. had at sea or across the ocean. Other conservatives, especially in the U.S., began to rediscover the virtues of nuclear deterrence and to dig in. But as long as the anti-nuclear Ronald Reagan was in office they could not dig in too far, so the yawning gap within the alliance had to be papered over. In accepting the "second zero" at their own meeting in Reykjavik in June 1987, NATO foreign ministers also came together on a formula for sequential arms-control negotiations involving Europe that called for establishment of a new conventional balance and the global elimination of chemical weapons before negotiations on the "third zero" could even begin.

Just before the Reagan Administration ended, in January 1989 the old CSCE trade-off between security and human rights was reenacted in the conclusion of the Vienna CSCE Review Conference. But now the Soviets and the West each saw their advantage in forward movement on *both* security and human rights, with little dissent from their allies and significant reservations only from Romania, on human rights. Vienna produced a document that committed the CSCE countries to major human rights improvements and a human rights conference in Moscow in 1991; in arms control, it committed them to two new negotiations on conventional arms control in Europe, one on confidence-building measures, one on force reductions. So negotiations on conventional arms were now front and center on the East-West agenda. But *still* the West Germans kept pushing to begin negotiations for the third nuclear zero. The superpower relationship was more stable; there was progress on nuclear arms control; but as East-West tension abated, West-West tension rose. And it created two new and major political questions.

One question was addressed to the incoming Bush Administration in Washington, and had to do with American leadership. Here the question was how to stay ahead of Gorbachev. The other question was addressed to the Western Alliance as a whole: If the military confrontation in Europe was fading, what was NATO for? Even if the whole elaborate structure of deterrence built up over so many years could be kept in place, even if political support could be maintained for the necessary defense expenditures, what was the Alliance's purpose? In harsh political terms, to keep the structure and maintain the support that purpose had to be defined.

In the spring of 1989 the Bush Administration arrived at a single answer to both questions. When he came to Europe in May, the President proposed to NATO that it rededicate itself to ending the division of Europe. Its first priority would be to negotiate a new conventional balance that would eliminate the disparities and asymmetries which had favored the Soviets for two generations and which the Soviets had built up in order to protect the Stalinist regimes they had imposed in Eastern Europe. But the Alliance's larger goal, inside and outside such negotiations, was now political. It was not there just to deter military attack; it was there to bring divided Europe back together, whole and free. And NATO agreed.

Six weeks later, in Paris in July, Gorbachev announced that he too agreed: East and West should now focus their energies on ending the division of Europe. The President then underlined his message by visiting Poland and Hungary, the two East European countries most earnestly engaged in political reform. And he went from there to mobilize the economic support of the other major industrialized nations for Polish and Hungarian reform efforts, conditional on their continuation. Gathered in Paris a week after Gorbachev's visit to celebrate the bicentennial of the French Revolution, the other Western and Japanese leaders climbed on board and put East-West relations in Europe front and center on their agenda, even ahead of the environmental and North-South issues they had advertised. And once again Gorbachev was willing to play, and made it easier for them with a surprise letter suggesting that a reforming Soviet Union now deserved to join their international economic system.

Such, I think, were the separate paths that the two superpowers and their European allies took to reach the common denominator of agreement that it was time to tackle the division of the continent where the Cold War began. It had taken them a whole decade to get there, and they still had a lot of work ahead of them. What got them there had something to do with trust and confidence. But it had much more to do with the pursuit of discrete national interests as they were defined by each player at every step. For my part, I am convinced that that is also what it will take to move from this new common base to the specific steps it will take to end the Cold War. What I have given you is, after all, history. It cannot be repeated, and it cannot be trusted to carry us forward by sheer inertia toward the goal we have set for ourselves, or any other goal. But at least by the end of the decade it had gotten us to the beginnings of a new deal for Europe. And that was already a great deal.

Chapter 7

Reflections on the End of the Cold War

I n the preceding pages I have tried to tell the story of
what has happened to the Cold War over these past ten
years. It is a story still very much imbedded in the Cold
War, still very much a part of its time. The countries involved in the story still defined problems and sought to
solve them in ways that would favor their own interests.
To be sure, each player naturally sought to define objectives in terms that went beyond narrow national problems
and goals, in language that others could understand and
agree to. Hence ideals were very much part of the story.
When asked whether I thought players were sincere in
promoting those ideals, I have found it wise to give them
all the benefit of the doubt. But it remains true that actual
developments, actual decisions, were shaped less by these
ideals than by specific interests in specific situations.

It was to resolve specific American dilemmas that the
Reagan Administration fashioned a new American policy

approach in Soviet affairs; built that approach into a concrete negotiating program; and discovered that America had recovered enough strength and confidence to begin real negotiations under that program, if the Soviets were willing. It was in the context of specific Soviet dilemmas that the new Gorbachev leadership turned to summitry in relations with the United States; that it finally accepted the American four-part agenda for dialogue; that it proposed the Reykjavik meeting; that it turned to political reform at home; that it decided process was the name of the game in superpower relations; and that the INF Treaty became an arms-control result sufficient to validate that process politically. To resolve specific dilemmas, certain East European countries turned to political reform in the 1980s; the Helsinki process became a living instrument for transacting international business; conventional arms control became an urgent international issue; and at the end of the decade East and West decided it was time to tackle the division of Europe they had lived with for two generations. Each step was intended to deal with a current dilemma, and each step in turn created a new situation with its own new dilemmas. At each step every player acted in pursuit of particular interests conceived in the classic terms we had all inherited: ideals, to be sure, but also group interests, and above all national interests. In that sense, nothing had changed.

And yet something has changed. Because the players did more or less well in the 1980s, it is now possible to look at the decade and at the Cold War itself as history. To me at least, history is a record of contingent actions taken by nations and groups to define and deal with concrete, time-driven problems. Living men and women make it up as they go along; history is the story of how they did so. Talented people have tried before to think about the Cold War as history. If they were unsuccessful, it is because until now we have all been in the thrall of the reasons why the Cold War was necessary, why it was destiny. I hope to have at least suggested the possibility of putting that destiny behind us at last. I hope having that possibility before us will also make it easier for us to think ahead. So in this last chapter I would like to share some thoughts about where this history is leading us.

It could lead us away from the terrors of our terrible century. Measured against the length of human lives, a century is not a very long time. There are those among us who can recall when the First World War began, who can remember when there was no Cold War. My father and my mother-in-law were both born in 1903 and can recollect such a time. My mother-in-law is now writing out some recollections of her life, and in one of them she describes what it was like to live in 1942 near Galveston, Texas, with her two little girls and her husband, who was in army training to go overseas. And from her stories of incident and adventure, a sentence leapt off the page at me. It read, "And at camp the routine of preparing men for slaughter went on." In those days war was unnatural. Mobilization, adventure, slaughter were not part of the American order of things. They were accepted and endured, but they were something to be done and gotten over with. They were not enduring features of the human landscape. They were *caused*. They were not destiny.

It is, of course, not true that only a sense of history produces right conduct. Americans often do the right thing without any sense of history at all, and they are not alone. Most of the players in the story I have told accepted the Cold War as destiny and acted for very current and very ahistorical purposes. Yet they conducted themselves well enough to permit us at last to consider what they did as history. And once you begin to look at human events as an infinite series of contingent actions for specific cause, it becomes easier to identify and weigh future possibilities and to take actions for good cause.

And still, we must be very careful. Part of the lesson is that history does not exist, or work, by itself. It is not something that is simply there and true. It is not just an objective record of past events that all reasonable men and women of goodwill can understand, and must accept when they do. Just as real men and women create the record by taking actions for various contingent purposes, so real men and women fashion history. They pick and choose what they consider significant to record; they leave out what they consider insignificant in that record. And they fashion that history, and use it, for various purposes. They *can* use it as a form of human understanding, as an aid to better conduct. That is the way I have tried to use it here. But they certainly do use it as a political weapon, as a construct intended to impel or prevent political movement in various directions. And nowhere is this truer than in East-West affairs.

The fact that history is used that way is important for the future of the Cold War. In East-West relations history is not only liberation from destiny. It is also one practical way of projecting and promoting political hopes for the future, one way of embodying political values in concrete political competition. In the years ahead, it seems to me that competition is likely to be more and more concerned with values and less and less with military security issues or with economic competitiveness.

I think this will be the case across the whole northern hemisphere, both within countries and between East and West. And history, with its uses and misuses, is likely to be one of the key vehicles in that competition over values.

The reasons are complex, and have as much to do with the social function of values as with their intrinsic power or appeal. For most of the postwar period, beginning in the 1950s, in all developed industrial countries politics was mainly "about" economics. In North America, in Western Europe, in Eastern Europe, in the Soviet Union, political struggle was over how to divide up pieces of a constantly growing economic pie among various political claimants. More or less stable economic growth came to seem natural, part of the way things are. This growth was based on traditional manufacturing, so that each country had a stable or growing industrial working class. These working classes in turn defined the issues of politics. As long as there was economic growth that satisfied their aspirations for upward social mobility and increasing material welfare or at least made those aspirations seem realistic, political competition was about the management of growth. Politicians who focused on values were labeled "extremist" and regularly lost. Every system produced its own ideology to express and accommodate that reality. They were all varieties of what I have labeled economism, the insistence that the state of the economy was really the main political issue. With our American flair for exaggeration, we discovered the "end of ideology" itself, thereby subtracting a politics of values from the very definition of politics. In Western Europe there were various ideological melds of the free market and the welfare state. In the East there were various forms of "goulash communism" or "social compact," trade-offs between rising living standards and political quiescence. All these ideologies had the same effect: They depoliticized politics.

In our time, however, all these ideologies are losing their political grip, for solid social and political reasons. The information revolution is transforming all our economies. Stable economic growth is harder and harder to produce. It depends more and more on the production of knowledge rather than the production of things. Manufacturing production is constant or increasing, but the cost of materials in products is plummeting, and manufacturing employment is declining everywhere. This is in turn destroying the working classes that defined political aspirations throughout the developed world. The institutions that gave shape to politics — trade unions, political parties, states — are losing their credibility and authority. Politicians are no longer able to promise stable economic growth, and they must therefore compete for political leadership in some other way. Increasingly they have had to try to build coalitions issue by issue, in order to appeal to increasingly diffuse and floating populations. And this can be done only by appealing to values.

The trend toward a politics of values seems as clear to me in Gorbachev's Soviet Union or Jaruzelski's Poland as in Margaret Thatcher's Britain or Ronald Reagan's America. But at this point the differences between East and West become very significant again, for a brand of politics whose focus is values rather than economic efficiency has very different effects on each side of the East-West divide. In general, the Communist world is still less industrialized, less urbanized, more agricultural than the West. All other things being equal, this could mean that economistic politics have more staying power in the East. And, in fact, that could still be true in areas where classic Stalinist industrialization can still appeal to underemployed peasants or first-generation workers and the raw party patronage machines that derive from them and drive them. I am thinking of Slovakia, say, or Romania, or Bulgaria, or Soviet Central Asia. But all other things are *not* equal. Stalinist economism may not be exhausted as an engine for economic growth and political control in every area of the Communist world. But everywhere in the East, both in the less and in the more developed regions, Stalinism's four decades of dominion have had a peculiar greenhouse effect on the staying power of values.

Stalinism has sought for over forty years to abolish what we in the West define as politics and to *impose* economics as the sole legitimate topic of political debate. Not only did it not succeed, it was literally counter-productive: Repression kept traditional political values almost perfectly preserved and very much alive, if not well. Repression often has this effect. The Communist countries are not the only area in today's world where economic issues are ceasing to be the stuff of politics, or where they are being joined or replaced by ethical and moral values. In all our industrialized countries we must expect to see and deal with a resurgence of the traditional values that have been most repressed in the era of economism. Our American industrial working class is also shrinking, and our electorate is also becoming more mobile than before. Patriotic and religious values, neo-conservatism, neo-Protestantism, also have a larger place in American politics. "Social issues" — school prayer, abortion, the flag — are moving up on our national agenda too. But it is in the Soviet Union and Eastern Europe that traditional values have been *most* repressed. And when and as the Stalinist icepack thaws and shifts and splinters in these countries, traditional values are likely to surge up through the cracks with a force that is hard for us to imagine.

This does not mean that the political systems of the East cannot handle them. But it does mean that traditional values will be harder to handle there than here. In our liberal democratic politics, debate over values never disappeared even at the height of economism, because debate is part of our system. Now our debate over values will be stronger, but we have the mechanisms, the institutions, to handle it. By contrast, in the Communist world Stalinism discredited the very concept of rational debate and decision over issues and programs using agreed mechanisms. It claimed to be replacing arbitrary, personalized rule exercised by self-appointing, self-perpetuating bureaucracies. For the mass of the populations in Eastern Europe and the Soviet Union, politics was traditionally an elite function, something someone else did. The best you could hope for as a subject was a virtuous leader, or a leader more virtuous than the scoundrels in place, someone who would give the little man a better break. Politics was a matter of ethics rather than a matter of efficiency. Most people saw programs as scams and shams that masked corrupt personal interest. Populations judged leaders not by whether they were likely to be effective in moving the country in a given direction but by whether they were good or bad men. Stalinism said it was replacing this moralistic politics with the modern brand, a brand oriented toward programs, toward efficiency. But in trying to do so it was obliged to put the children of family-oriented peasants in power, and they reproduced and reinforced the bad old politics every bit as much as they replaced it. The result has been a tremendous hodgepodge, and the populations as a whole remained firmly attached to the concept that politics is really "about" morals.

History is one of Western man's favorite ways to exemplify morals. It is therefore one of the main political footballs of the Communist world. One of the great questions in each country's politics is who best represents the national values inherited from the past. It is not a new question. Stalinism preserved the national frameworks, and every Communist regime has sought to co-opt the national history to shore up its shaky legitimacy. The economization of the East-West competition that I have described increased the opportunities for regimes to nationalize themselves because it depoliticized the contest. So both in its flowering in the 1960s and its decay in the 1970s, economism generated a revival of national values and national political problematics. But that has just made the struggle over who owns the national past more bitter as economism has declined. Saving the national past from the regime is one of the major objectives of political opposition whenever it is permitted to raise its voice. So calls for the truth, the whole truth and nothing but the truth — about the past — echo through the area today. The regimes are summoned to admit their lies and replace the evil men who lied, and they respond by replacing men and bargaining over the historical truth. For example, the 1939 Molotov-Ribbentrop Pact consigning the Baltic Republics to the Soviet Union is a major issue between them and Moscow. But this is only one example among many. Much of the politics of the Communist world today consists of just such competition over who owns the national past between discredited Stalinism rationalism and resurgent moralism.

There is no necessary reason why such competition should stop in any given Communist country. But there is also no necessary reason why it should go on forever until one side or the other emerges triumphant to relish the tears in its enemy's eyes. And in some countries efforts are, in fact, underway to transcend it, to go beyond competition about the past and put in place what we would consider genuine political debate about current issues and programs. That, as I take it, is the significance of the recent political evolution we have seen in Poland, Hungary, and parts of the European USSR. The returns are not yet in. In each of these countries politics includes vigorous struggle over the past: in Poland, over who was responsible for the sins of the 1970s and 1980s, not to speak of earlier periods; in Hungary, over the interpretation of the 1956 revolt and where to bury the ashes of Imre Nagy and other martyrs; in the Soviet Union over the Stalin question, and now a variety of national issues, including the status of Nagorno-Karabakh in the Caucasus, and the Molotov-Ribbentrop Pact just mentioned. Nevertheless, each of these countries has been driven by its own political dynamics to go beyond the past. In each we seen an emerging new thematics oriented toward the present and the future as well, and an opening up of the political system to accommodate it.

The effect of this onset of the present and future is diversification of the ex-"Communist Bloc" on a scale that Western Cold War policymakers could only dream of. This diversification goes quite beyond simple resurgence of national issues in relations among Communist states or divergent national approaches to economic and political issues that are important in East-West relations. Even at that level diversity makes it harder for the Soviet writ to run throughout the area, and thus for the Soviets to mobilize the area's resources for their own purposes. But the diversification we are now witnessing is a larger phenomenon, in its magnitude and — if it continues — in its potential consequences for the international system.

Diversification in the Communist world is no longer just a matter of national symbolism or specific policies within a basically uniform Stalinist structure. It now extends to fundamental features of the structure itself. Communist countries are becoming different from each other in their institutions, in their ways of defining and pursuing objectives, in the objectives they pursue. Much Western commentary focuses on the danger for the international system of crisis in Eastern Europe. I think much of that commentary has already been overtaken by events on the ground. The return of politics in Communist countries may well lead to crisis in individual countries. But because they are now so different from each other, it is becoming harder and harder for the Soviets or anyone else to define a systemic bottom line, a "red line" beyond which intervention is necessary to save the system. There may well be such a red line. The Soviets are currently refusing to define one, but I take this to be a matter of policy rather than necessity; they could define one if they had to. The point is that it is getting genuinely harder to define. As a result, crisis in one part of the Communist world no longer means that the whole system is in jeopardy. Crisis in one country is therefore much less likely to provoke a reaction from the Soviet Union and other Communist countries, and thereby to spill over into the international system. We do not know what the future will bring, but we already know that systemic change is numbering the days of the Brezhnev Doctrine.

However, other potential international consequences of Communist-world diversification cut in a different direction. If diversity continues to grow on the scale we have been seeing, the Cold War reasons why we cared at all about what happened in the Communist world will lose their force. I believe the demilitarization of the East-West confrontation in Europe is a variable that is largely independent of political change within the East. If the military confrontation in Europe abates, it will be because Soviet and Western leaders are trying to overcome current policy dilemmas that have little to do with Eastern Europe. But demilitarization does erode the East-West rationale for stationing large Soviet forces in Eastern Europe. And systemic diversification erodes the "policing" function of these forces, the need to keep them there to defend Communist regimes. They may be left with no strong rationale at all. For us in the West, these forces have been one large component of the Soviet military threat that has been an anchor of the Cold War. As the anchor starts to drift, we in the West will care less about the troubled waters on the other side.

We will also have less incentive to expand East-West economic relations. This is paradoxical, because one reason the Communist regimes are reforming themselves is that they wish once again to attract the economic resources which the West once used to compete for political influence in Eastern Europe, but which dried up in the 1970s. Where political reform is taking place, it is designed in part precisely to underpin economic reform that will make these economies competitive and appealing to Western partners. It could indeed have that effect over the long term. But in the short term the transitions to new forms of political and economic management are not only politically contentious but also economically disruptive. Economic disruption will make these economies less rather than more attractive partners for Western firms and governments. And even over the longer term the prognosis is not good. The small, jumbled economies of Eastern Europe lack the resources to compete at the cutting edge of the information revolution. On economic grounds alone the most likely prospect for them is marginalization, and their best prospect is sub-contracting for larger, more efficient economic units, doing piecework for Western Europe, or Japan, or us. So on economic as well as military grounds we will have less reason to care about what happens in the Communist world.

Why then should we care at all? To paraphrase Neville Chamberlain during the Munich crisis, why should we continue to direct our attention and engage our resources in what is happening in these faraway countries, among these peoples about whom we know nothing? The answer, I think, is two-fold.

First, simple caution enjoins us to stay interested. We have a large interest in seeing many of the changes under-way made irreversible. But it is also true that most of them are still reversible. This is particularly true of Soviet change, and the Soviet Union is still a military superpower and a big, strong, resourceful country that retains the capacity to threaten our interests very seriously. Reform in Poland and Hungary in the direction of greater political pluralism and more market-oriented economic arrange-ments is important, because it diversifies the Communist world and brings the two parts of divided Europe closer. But in Poland, Hungary, and eventually elsewhere in East-ern Europe, such reform has a reliable future only if the

Soviet Union goes down the same path and keeps going down it. Diversity within the Communist world is not new. What is new, and what is significant in terms of ending the Cold War, is diversity within the Soviet Union.

At the end of that path lies a Europeanization of the Soviet Union, or important parts of it, that will change the character of the Soviet polity itself. I think it is fair to say that such a process is underway. The brand of politics we see emerging in large sectors of the European USSR seems to me to have more in common with Polish or Hungarian politics than it does with the politics still practiced in the rest of the country, or in much of Communist southeastern Europe. In Moscow, in the Baltic Republics, in parts of the Russian Federation, men and women are organizing themselves in number to debate and struggle over programs as well as over symbols, just as they now do in Warsaw and Budapest, and as they do not yet do in Tbilisi, or Yerevan, or Bucharest, or for that matter in Yugoslav Macedonia. In Moscow we see in the elite the same magic triangle, as it has been called, of top-down reformers, Communist populists, and stand-pat *apparatchiki*, all of them trying to stay ahead of the wave that is carrying traditional values to the forefront of politics. They compete to adopt and co-opt it where they can, they combat it where they must. If such change continues, the Soviet empire will be a different empire even if it stays an empire. But change in that direction will be a very much longer and more intricate process than similar processes in Eastern European countries; it will be even more contentious, and its outcome is by no means certain.

There is also little we Americans can do as a country to influence the outcome decisively. Nevertheless, we should care about that prospect, and I am confident that we will care, for a second, different reason, one over which we have more control. We Americans too are leaving the economistic age and returning to a politics of values. We consider pluralism, democracy, the rule of law, free-market economics to be not just efficient but precious. Our reasons for supporting them go beyond the practical; they go to the core of our belief systems. We will now care more about them than ever. And today, outside the Western world, the practical preconditions for putting such values into practice are nowhere stronger than in the Communist world. By world standards the countries now in it are economically developed. Their educational revolutions have produced large proto-middle classes that are now starting to find an end to arbitrary rule politically attractive. The state systems of the area overwhelmed democracy when they were Stalinist, but they should be strong enough to support democracy if dictatorship is dismantled, which is not true everywhere in the world. So even without the Soviet military threat and even without economic incentives, we in the West have powerful reasons to care and to engage what resources we can in a promising cause.

We can and will contribute to the process of change in the East, therefore. Our own political system is the most open in the world. We Americans weave together politics, economics, and culture together more habitually than others do. Even our concept of nationality is based on values, or what we choose to be, rather than on attributes, or the characteristics we were born with. We have much to offer the changing Communist world.

But in plunging into the thicket of values politics in the East we must realize that we are entering a world of competing golden ages that are often foreign to us. There is nothing un-American about moving forward in politics by seeking to re-create a better past. To its adherents, the Reagan revolution was, after all, meant to be a restoration. And there will be an attractive overlap between the moral and ethical values of oppositionists in Communist countries striving to return to a better past and an American policy of encouraging progress toward a more democratic future. But that overlap is partly real and partly fictitious. If it is democratic, the golden age in these countries is partly fictitious, and if it is real, it is only partly democratic. In Eastern Europe and the Soviet Union, democratic institutions and habits of mind belong more to the present and even more to the future than to the past. The past, and therefore the future, is really up for grabs.

Once Stalinism dies as destiny and becomes history, it becomes possible to offer competing visions. At the same time, by suppressing competition Stalinism gave tremendous ethical purity and political force to a whole series of older visions or utopias. Among Communists there is great nostalgia for the last pre-Stalinist period. In the Soviet Union that means the 1920s, the period of the New Economic Policy or NEP, when the Bolsheviks commanded the political and economic heights but allowed considerable initiative from below. In Eastern Europe it means the period from 1944 to 1948 , when other parties and various forms of property were legal and competed with the Communists and socialist property. In both the Soviet Union and Eastern Europe there is accordingly a Communist vision of the Party as a real party, capable of competing in an open political arena by political means rather than Stalinist force. Among non-Communists there are visions of the last pre-Communist regime, or the last pre-Communist and pre-authoritarian regime. In Russia this leads back to the silver age before World War I, to the world of Solzhenitsyn's *August 1914*, or the world of *Pamyat'*. In the non-Russian republics it leads to the twilight of independence before the Bolsheviks came. In Eastern Europe it leads to the interwar period.

To be sure, when it comes to political competition, all these visions have their work cut out for them. The non-Communist pasts have been discredited not only by decades of hostile regime propaganda but by the passage of time and in a number of cases also by association with foreign powers. In Russia the pre-Communist world is very distant indeed, and before communism the non-Russian nations of the area, inside and outside the USSR, were weak and dependent. If they did not depend directly on foreign powers, as did Croatia and Slovakia and the various quisling movements of World War II, then they depended on foreign capital, as did Romania. Conservative nostalgics did not do at all well in the recent Soviet and Polish election campaigns, and for once it was not because they were repressed. Even in the 1980s age of iron the pre-Communist pasts are not very attractive politically.

176

But neither are the Communist pasts. The Soviet 1920s are also very distant, and there have been achievements since then, such as industrialization and winning the war, of which most Soviets are proud. The argument is about the cost of the achievements rather than the achievements themselves. The 1944-48 period in Eastern Europe is closer in time, but it is just close enough for people to remember and to have passed on to their children that it was nasty and brutish as well as short; that the decks were completely stacked; and that all the so-called free competition and multi-party struggle that some Communist populists are so nostalgic for took place under the anxious eye of the Western embassies, to be sure, but mainly under the heavy wings of the NKVD and the Red Army.

It is true that Communist and authoritarian models are not the only ones the past offers. Several countries of the area had authentic democratic experience — the Czech lands come to mind — and those who offer it as a model deserve respect. But no one has any serious idea of what kind of social and political support such models or visions from the past would generate in free political competition. The lesson, I think, is that we should be very careful about models as such. It is only by transcending these models and going beyond them to the slow, patient, demanding work of developing contemporary programs and institutions for defining and managing national issues that the Stalinist past will be finally overcome.

I myself think that goes for our model too. We believe that liberal democracy in politics and the free market in economics are functionally interrelated, that they depend on and support each other. Our idea that this linked system is the proper alternative to Stalinism in the Communist world is as old as the Cold War. It has been *the* Western model on offer.

In the early years it somehow lacked the cutting edge of plausibility in Eastern Europe. It was controversial within Western Europe itself. We should remember that even in Britain consensus in favor of it firmed up only in the 1950s. The United States was, in fact, the only working model, and aside from being distant and special, to Western Europe we were a baby-faced giant, and in the Stalinist East we were imperialist Uncle Sam. Moreover, liberal democracy and the market were blamed all over the East for having let Hitler happen and by extension for the destruction and suffering he wrought. Finally, the East was being told that Stalinism was its working destiny. Force-fed industrialization under Communist rule was to be the remedy for backwardness and weakness, and anyway there was no choice.

That has changed, but it has not been the carriers of the liberal free-market ideal who have changed it, although they have helped keep the concept alive. Rather, the choice has been re-created by the comparison between Eastern and Western performance, in terms not just of freedom but of equity and productive efficiency. More specifically, it has been re-created by the failure of the Stalinist regimes in their own terms and the relative success of market-based democracy, chastened but still liberal, in Western Europe. It is that contrast which has brought democratic market-oriented liberalism back as a competitor, in the guise of civil society and market socialism.

Yet it is premature to say that it has triumphed, as some now do. As Lincoln put it in his second Inaugural Address, "The prayers of both could not be answered. That of neither has been answered fully." I do not believe the contest is over, not in military terms, not in systemic terms, not even in value terms. It seems to me that some form of socialism, or various forms of what could still be called socialism, are still in the running. In the reforming Eastern countries, one objective of reform is to create a *new* kind of socialism. It is still undefined, but it would be different from either our Western model or from Stalinism. Gorbachev and his group, other top-down reformers in other countries, and the Communist populists who are emerging in uneasy partnership with them are all trying to save socialism rather than bury it. Right now they appear to be calling in democrats as counterweights to the nationalists who are also surging forward as politics opens up. But that does not change the objective: They are still trying to throw ballast, to jettison the unessential, Stalinist parts of socialism — if they can only be defined politically as unessential — in order to save the rest. I believe the Soviet Union is likely to remain messianic in its approach to national interests and objectives, to define for itself a special mission of universal relevance. It will be less dangerous as a country, perhaps. But it will still be ambitious and visionary, even if the vision is now democratic rather than Stalinist socialism.

Many outcomes are conceivable. A return to Stalinism is one of the least likely. To give just an example of another, more plausible outcome, we could see a kind of dual economy emerge. It would put together a heavy industrial sector run by the nomenclatura along traditional lines with a free-market sector that would be open to all but dominated by the nomenclatura and their children. The private sector would be tributary to the socialized sector, from which it would have to get its inputs through personal connections in the same way that peasants produce the eggs and milk on their private plots using grain stolen from the collectivized fields. In the large Soviet economy this could be tried on a territorial basis, with the Baltic Republics allowed to operate free economies within the larger economy. In a smaller economy like Poland's, the division of labor would be sectoral, with much of heavy industry still socialist but with services joining agriculture in private hands. The political system that would fit such a dual economy could not be Stalinist. It would have to be less centralized and more supple. It would probably be freer and more pluralistic in order to manage such an unwieldy economic organism. But it would also be very different from ours.

What does this mean for us? It means first of all that we would be wise to resist triumphalism. Triumphalism is as American as apple pie, and there is nothing wrong with that. But up to now no triumph of the kind some are now celebrating has been permanent, and the mornings after are always hard. Those mornings after can also be dangerous, because disillusionment produces the pendulum swings that have infected the American approach to the Communist world since there was one, and thus American policy. We too will remain a messianic great power, and our vision of the good life and the good international order has much to contribute to the emerging politics of the Communist world. The increasing political importance of our values in our own politics will keep us interested. I am confident we will stay in the game. But the game will go on.

If we are in for the long haul, however, what should we base our policy on? I believe we should also resist basing it either on analysis alone or on vision alone.

The trouble with analysis is that Communist-world politics will remain both secretive and different from ours, so that we will never know enough or understand enough to fine-tune our policies exactly to what is going on. Moreover, we are not even agile enough to try. We are a big and open political system, and to be sustainable at all American policy must develop slowly and must appeal to a broad spectrum of interests, including sectoral and special interests that could not care less about what is really going on in the Communist world. Good analysis can help avoid mistakes and can guide policy judgment in the right directions, but making it the sole basis of policy is a recipe for tripping over our own feet and tying ourselves in knots.

The trouble with vision is different, but has the same effect. In our system leaders must be seen to have vision, but no American vision ever quite fits the Communist world it is intended to shape, and each is also politically divisive in this country. Almost any number can play at vision, and in a diverse society with open politics like ours, if you try to base current policy on vision for the year 2000, say, you find yourself dealing with competing visions that clash in the arena of politics. Depending on the political outcome, you either narrow the political base for your policy or you invite policy deadlock. Every issue fought on the basis of vision conjures up Armageddon, and policymakers shy away from Armageddon, so the only decisions that can be made are those forced by outside agency, either foreign — some action by Gorbachev or our allies — or domestic — some political or electoral interest. Very often the policy reaction is either bad or no decision at all.

And yet I hope to have shown that even if we cannot base policy on analysis alone or vision alone, the United States also cannot leave everything to Gorbachev, or for that matter to history either. We will be obliged to contribute to the processes underway, and we have an important contribution to make. We will not be able to act with perfect agility on the basis of perfect understanding to promote a coherent vision. But we will contribute. I would submit that the way to do so is to try to pursue clearly defined U.S. values and interests vis-à-vis the Communist world. We should try to define objectives that are understood and accepted by the American electorate and that produce results which the electorate finds useful in terms of those interests. To define such objectives we will need both analysis and vision, but to be broadly understood and accepted the objectives themselves cannot be over-refined or over-ambitious. They should be stated in terms of directions, of movement toward goals, rather than proclaimed as ends in themselves. And they should be pursued as part of a continuous process of interaction and dialogue with the other side.

That, at any rate, is the way we have tried to do it over the past ten years, and I believe the history of the past ten years shows that it can be done. I would like to think that the interim result, the first fruit, has been a degree of convergence in the way the United States and its allies, and the Soviet Union and its allies, deal with foreign and domestic issues respectively. The Soviet Union and some other Communist countries are walking back from their traditional maximalism in domestic politics, the attempt to impose an end to history by force. In its place they are introducing some of the debate with the future open that is the staff of life in Western politics. And for its part the United States is getting used to a world where foreign policy cannot produce quick and final results. It is getting used to a world of process, of modest objectives and modest achievements in East-West relations. It is getting used to what President Kennedy called "the long, twilight struggle," the same struggle the Soviets have always conducted in foreign affairs. That, I think, is real convergence, and that, I think, is real progress.

If we are patient enough and wise enough to make that progress continue, I believe that the world our children and grandchildren live in will be better than the one we have grown up with and lived in under the Cold War. It will not be the world my father and mother-in-law knew when they were growing up. History cannot be repeated; the past cannot be recaptured in any politically significant sense. But if we continue, the world of the future will be closer to their world and better than ours. It will be more open, it will be freer, and, yes, it will be less militarized. The preparation of men for slaughter will have become unnatural once again. There will be less human suffering. It will take a long time, but it is a world worthy of our very best and most determined efforts to achieve.

It will not be the end of history. The proper analogy, I think, is with the change from the seventeenth to the eighteenth century. The seventeenth century in Europe and West Africa was a terrible century, as ours has been. It was not all bad — it settled these shores, for instance, and gave us the basics of our national development — but it was a bloody and ideological century indeed. It was the century that made Hobbes call human life nasty, brutish, and short. The eighteenth century was not all good — life remained nasty, brutish, and short in most places — but it was better. There was more peace, there was place for "new thinking," for new ideologies, and they were sunnier, more optimistic. They helped produce us, the American polity and the American dream. Of course, what they really did was help us produce ourselves, through a revolution, and then the French Revolution whose bicentennial we have just celebrated. And then the world was off and running again. But it was, I think, a better world. And I think that if we are determined, and wise, and patient, we too can help produce a world that much better. And that, I think, will be the end of the Cold War.

Index

909.82 Simons, Thomas W.
SIM   The end of the cold
               war?

$16.95   9/25/90

DATE		

I LONGWOOD
DATE DUE
05 13 96
DUE

LONGWOOD
DATE DUE
01 27 91